Book of Proverbs

Proverbs for the modern day

Donna Louis

DEDICATIONS AND ACKNOWLEDGMENTS

TO GOD OUR HEAVENLY FATHER WHO WAITED
PATIENTLY ON ME FOR SEVERAL YEARS TO FINALLY
ACCEPT AND FULFILL MY ASSIGNMENT.

TO MY HUSBAND PATRICK WHO IS A ROCK AND A
CONSTANT SUPPORTER OF MY WORK. I LOVE YOU.

TO DON WHO HELPED ME GO FROM INVISIBLE TO
VISIBLE. I COULD NEVER HAVE DONE IT WITHOUT YOU.
THANK YOU.

Table Of Contents

INTRODUCTION

Proverbs are a collection of moral sayings and counsels forming a book of Christian Scripture.

A proverb is practical; it presents counsel that is valuable and productive in the world today.

King David's son Solomon was the wisest man during his time.

The Book of Proverbs contains 31 chapters all with prudent sayings.

The wise sayings in Proverbs are divinely inspired.

The Book of Proverbs is meant to enrich your life with wisdom and understanding.

The Book of Proverbs sayings if applied correctly to your life with the fear of God will bless your life tremendously.

Are you the person who leans to their own understanding instead of seeking wisdom? Are you puzzled and discouraged about all the mistakes you have made?

One of the greatest gifts that a writer can receive is a greater understanding of what he or she is writing about. It has blessed me to say this happened while writing this book. I am no expert and honestly, nobody is. The only expert who walked the earth was Jesus Christ. We all just need to resolve daily to do better, be better, and let go and let God do the rest because we can do nothing on our own. Everything comes from him. Studying the Book of Proverbs needs to be a daily routine. Don't pressure yourself to learn it all in a month. Yes, there are 31 chapters in Proverbs, and you can always read chapters 30 and 31 in one day but repetition and routine take time. What takes even more time is to grasp the wisdom and understanding that the Book of Proverbs offers.

Don't chastise yourself if one of your weaknesses is always trying to figure things out. You have decided that you now want to trust God and let him handle everything because you are so tired of trying to fix things and instead of them getting better; they keep getting worse. However, you have been waiting on God to handle things and nothing has changed so you meddle in the situation again believing you can come to a perfect solution before God. He knows your impatience and will just sit back and wait until you realize you need to let him handle things no matter how long it takes. God knows what is in your heart and he will work with you. Remember that we are all on the potter's wheel and when God is finished molding us that is when we will be perfect and ready to enter heaven with Jesus Christ. May God bless you and yours as you read this book and read the Book of Proverbs, so you can embark on gaining wisdom and understanding that will bless your life.

Wisdom is the daughter of experience–Leonardo Da Vinci

Wisdom never comes to those who believe they have nothing left to learn–Charles De Lint

Intelligence is knowing the right answer, Wisdom is knowing when to say it–Tim Fargo

Turn your wounds into Wisdom–Oprah Winfrey

Cynicism is a sorry kind of Wisdom–Barack Obama

Knowledge speaks but Wisdom listens–Jimi Hendrix

Knowledge is horizontal, Wisdom is vertical, it comes down from above–Billy Graham

Don't gain the world and lose your soul, Wisdom is better than silver or gold–Bob Marley

The lotus is the most beautiful flower, whose petals open one by one. But it will only grow in the mud. In order to grow and gain wisdom, first you must have the mud --- the obstacles of life and its suffering. ... The mud speaks of the common ground that humans share, no matter what our stations in life. ... Whether we have it all or we have nothing, we are all faced with the same obstacles: sadness, loss, illness, dying and death. If we are to strive as human beings to gain more wisdom, more kindness and more compassion, we must have the intention to grow as a lotus and open each petal one by one. –Goldie Hawn

The Potter's Wheel–The Teacup

The story is told of a couple who went to England to celebrate their 25th wedding anniversary and shopped at a beautiful antique store. They both liked antiques and pottery, and especially teacups, and so spotting an exceptional cup, they asked "May we see that? We've never seen a cup quite so beautiful."

As the lady handed it to them, suddenly the teacup spoke... "You don't understand." It said, "I have not always been a teacup. There was a time when I was just a lump of red clay. My master took me and rolled me pounded and patted me over and over and I yelled out, don't do that. I don't like it!" "Let me alone," but he only smiled, and gently said; "Not yet!!" "Then, WHAM! I was placed on a spinning wheel and suddenly I was spun around and around and around." "Stop it! I'm getting so dizzy!" "I'm going to be sick!" I screamed.

But the master only nodded and said, quietly; 'Not yet.'

He spun me and poked and prodded and bent me out of shape to suit himself and then... he put me in the oven. I never felt such heat. I yelled and knocked and pounded at the door.

"Help! Get me out of here!" 'Not yet.' When I thought I couldn't bear it another minute, the door opened. He carefully took me out and put me on the shelf, and I began to cool.

Oh, that felt so good! "Ah, this is much better," I thought. But after I cooled, he picked me up, and he brushed and painted me all over. The fumes were horrible. "Oh, please, Stop it! Stop it!" I cried. He only shook his head and said. "Not yet..."

Then suddenly he put me back into the oven. Only it was not like the first time. This time it was twice as hot, and I just knew I would suffocate. I begged... I pleaded... I screamed... I cried... I was convinced I would never make it. I was ready to give up and just then the door opened, and he took me out and again placed me on the shelf, where I cooled and waited and waited, wondering "What's he going to do to me next?"

An hour later he handed me a mirror and said, "Look at yourself."

And I did... I said, "That's not me, that couldn't be me. It's beautiful. I'm beautiful!"

Quietly he spoke: "I want you to remember, then," he said, "I know it hurt to be rolled and pounded and patted, but had I just left you alone, you'd have dried up. I know it made you dizzy to spin around on the wheel, but if I had stopped, you would have crumbled."

"I know it hurt, and it was hot and disagreeable in the oven, but if I hadn't put you there, you would have cracked. I know the fumes were bad when I brushed and painted you all over, but if I hadn't done that, you never would have hardened. You would not have had any color in your life."

"And if I hadn't put you back in that second oven, you wouldn't have survived for long because the hardness would not have held. Now you are a finished product. Now you are what I had in mind when I first began with you."

Author Unknown

Chapter One

Proverbs 1:5

"A wise man will hear and will increase learning, and a man of understanding shall attain unto wise counsels."

When do people discontinue learning in life? According to King Solomon and the proverbs only an unwise man stops learning. A wise man will keep his ears open and decipher things he hears throughout his entire life and build upon his learning.

Let me say this to everyone right now the following statement I make you will see it repeated in this book many times. God gave all of us two ears and one mouth for a reason. He wants us to do more listening than talking. You cannot hear what someone else has to say or improve upon your listening and learning skills if your tongue is constantly in motion. So, a big part of learning how to become a person of wisdom is being quiet and being still.

The fool is the one who thinks he knows everything. These people are the ones that feel that have gained all the knowledge they will ever need. Unfortunately, that is an untrue assessment. The oldest living person in the Bible was Methuselah. He lived to be 969 years old and then he died. Even if we were to live that long we would never know all there is to know. Therefore, we should always be alert and ready to learn new things.

The second part of this proverb tells us that a person of understanding will gain good counsel. The more effort we put forth to hear and learn then we will gain a better understanding and wisdom. We will be able to differentiate between many things. When God sees us trying, he makes himself known to us which will make all the difference in the world.

Proverbs 1:7

"The fear of the Lord is the beginning of knowledge: but fools despise wisdom and instruction."

Wisdom - ability to discern inner qualities and relationships; a wise attitude, belief, or course of action.

Fear - an unpleasant often strong emotion caused by anticipation or awareness of danger; anxious concern.

Reverence - honor or respect felt or shown; a gesture of respect.

Awe - an emotion variously combining dread, veneration, and wonder that is inspired by authority or by the sacred or sublime.

Knowledge - the fact or condition of knowing something with familiarity gained through experience or association; the range of one's information or understanding. I am sure you have all heard the adage "knowledge is power." You can become powerful where the Lord is concerned in a fearful state. However, you must have the right fear which is reverential.

Above I have provided definitions of words critical to the Book of Proverbs and this verse. Wisdom means being wise and all of us can be that. To have knowledge of something it is mandatory we have familiarity and to do that we must have an association. We need to surround ourselves with that thing. Fear takes on all shapes and sizes. We can have a fear of roller coasters, airplanes, spiders, being alone, even being diagnosed with a deadly disease. Movies take on all genres but a film like Halloween and Friday the 13th inspire terror. To reverence something means to honor it. God specifically stated how important honor is in the book of Exodus 20:12, "Honor thy Father and Mother that thy days may be long upon the land which the Lord thy God giveth thee."

So now let's return to the above passage. The first part of this proverb is telling us we are to understand that the fear of the Lord is the beginning of knowledge. This is where it becomes tricky. We are not to have a fear of the Lord like we fear snakes, bees, etc. We are to have a reverential fear of the Lord. To fear God means we recognize him as supreme and absolute. This means we respect, honor, and we are to be in awe of the Lord. Why is this necessary? Well, first they state it in the above proverb. All things have their origin in God. Read Genesis Chapter 1. It states that God created the earth and everything in it. With that awesome power, we need to fear the Lord.

Proverbs 1:22

"How long, ye simple ones, will ye love simplicity? and the scorners delight in their scorning, and fools hate knowledge?"

3

In this proverb, Solomon is addressing three types of people in a disparaging way. It is downright insulting. He refers to the simple ones (simplicity) which imply ignorance. It satisfies lazy people just eating, working, playing, and sleeping. Do you lead a very basic life? Are you content to leave the mental work to others? This will never give you wisdom.

Scorners are people who despise and reject the truth. These people don't believe in building up others just tearing them down. These people live a lifestyle where they can offer nothing positive. They eventually become galling, people who are only concerned with their own desires who have nothing to offer anyone.

Finally, fools are people who lack good sense or judgment. I personally don't believe anyone wants to be described in that fashion. How do we make sure we steer clear from being categorized in this fashion? We crave wisdom! In the same way, people crave ballpark food at a sporting event like baseball. Oh, and for those people who follow baseball remember three strikes you're out so in this instance you would be called out by the home plate umpire and sent back to the dugout if you fall into these three categories.

Proverbs 1:26

"I also will laugh at your calamity; I will mock when your fear cometh."

Foolish people believe they know everything so if anyone tries to instruct them, they laugh. They go through life like it is a constant carnival or party and show contempt if anybody tries to take away their amusement and enjoyment. This is when God sits high in heaven and looks down below and laughs at them.

God is not someone to be mocked. He will have his day where the foolish are concerned. "He that sitteth in the heavens shall laugh: the Lord shall have them in derision."–Psalm 2:4. "The Lord shall laugh at him: for he seeth that his day is coming."–Psalm 37:13.

For, those of us who are mature enough to remember The Three Stooges show we know how happy Curly became once any bad thing or suffering happened to Moe. Unfortunately, Moe always thought he was better than Curly & Larry and so when he was deflated at any time, they both reveled in his bad fortune. Well, this is the same principle that this verse implies. Wisdom will laugh at your negative circumstances and make fun of your catastrophes because you felt you didn't need wisdom.

Proverbs 1:31

"Therefore, shall they eat of the fruit of their own way, and be filled with their own devices."

The above verse is saying in plain terms you deserve what you get because of bad decisions. In today's world, most people are reaping what they sowed because they made foolish choices. God has warned us in his word that we will be blessed if we do what he says and cursed if we don't.

Unfortunately, people today worldwide look at God and his words with contempt feeling it is worthless. Many people are only interested in what feels good to them. Feelings, however, can get you in a world of trouble. When we operate out of our flesh, we make many mistakes and that drives us to do ungodly things. There are many deeds of the flesh some of which are immorality, impurity, sensuality, idolatry, sorcery, enmities, strife, jealousy, anger, drunkenness and others.

A great example of making bad choices and then reaping the results would be this. If you are a person who has food allergies and is allergic to items like crabs, shrimp, clams, mussels, oysters, scallops, and shellfish then you need to stay clear of these things unless you want to be diagnosed with Anaphylaxis. This is a hypersensitivity as to foreign proteins or drugs resulting from sensitization following prior contact with the causative agent. This can manifest as hives, itching, and watery eyes. A good example of this would be the movie "Hitch" with Will Smith. Wisdom will keep you away from making bad decisions.

Chapter Two

Proverbs 2:3

"Yea, if thou criest after knowledge, and liftest up thy voice for understanding."

When you don't know what to do, you need to drop to your knees and cry out to God. Cry out to God for the ability to decipher the difference between things. Do you pray for wisdom? God has all wisdom, and He gives it to those who ask.

How often do you pray for knowledge? When was the last time you prayed for wisdom? If you do not ask God for it, you will never receive it. "Ask, and it shall be given you; seek, and ye shall find; knock, and it shall be opened unto you."–Matthew 7:7.

Wisdom and knowledge are something you should earnestly pray for. King Solomon did. "And Solomon loved the Lord, walking in the statutes of David his father: only he sacrificed and burnt incense in high places. And the king went to Gibeon to sacrifice there; for that was the great high place: a thousand burnt offerings did Solomon offer upon that altar. In Gibeon the Lord appeared to Solomon in a dream by night: and God said, ask what I shall give thee. And Solomon said, thou hast shewed unto thy servant David my father great mercy, according as he walked before thee in truth, and in righteousness, and in uprightness of heart with thee; and thou hast kept for him this great kindness, that thou hast given him a son to sit on his throne, as it is this day. And now, O Lord my God, thou hast made thy servant king instead of David my father: and I am but a little child: I know not how to go out or come in. And thy servant is in the midst of thy people which thou hast chosen, a great people, that cannot be numbered nor counted for multitude. Give therefore thy servant an understanding heart to judge thy people, that I may discern between good and bad: for who is able to judge this thy so great a people? And the speech pleased the Lord, that Solomon had asked this thing. And God said unto him, Because thou hast asked this thing, and hast not asked for thyself long life; neither hast asked riches for thyself, nor hast asked the life of thine enemies; but hast asked for thyself understanding to discern judgment; Behold, I have done according to thy words: lo, I have given thee a wise and an understanding heart; so that there was none like thee before thee, neither after thee shall any arise like unto thee. And I have also given thee that which thou hast not asked, both riches, and honour: so that there shall not be any among the kings like unto thee all thy days. And if thou wilt walk in my ways, to keep my statutes and my commandments, as thy father David did walk, then I will lengthen thy days."–1 Kings 3:3-14.

When we cry out and lift our voice regarding something, we are making an earnest plea. If we earnestly want knowledge and understanding that will keep us away from a lot of disappointment and sorrow.

Proverbs 2:7

"He layeth up sound wisdom for the righteous: he is a buckler to them that walk uprightly."

Wisdom is the foundation of security and safety. If we will walk righteously God will be our buckler. The Lord has all the wisdom in the world, but He has made plenty available for good people.

What is a buckler? It is a shield. "The sons of Reuben, and the Gadites, and half the tribe of Manasseh, of valiant men, men able to bear buckler and sword, and to shoot with bow, and skilful in war, were four and forty thousand seven hundred and threescore, that went out to the war."–1 Chronicles 5:18. "Thy neck is like the tower of David builded for an armoury, whereon there hang a thousand bucklers, all shields of mighty men."–Song of Solomon 4:4.

Now everyone who has ever worn a belt knows what the purpose is and what it does, and this is what God says he will do for us. He will keep us lifted above all the mess.

Proverbs 2:11

"Discretion shall preserve thee, understanding shall keep thee."

In today's world, a vast number of people purchase a security system. They do this because they want to lower the risks that what they own will remain safe and protected. They also do it, so they can rest comfortably at ease when they retire to sleep.

When we use wisdom, we live with prudence. An ungodly person doesn't let prudence guide them. They don't think about what the result will be they do as they choose.

Let's define discretion—the quality of being careful about what you do and say so that people will not feel embarrassed or offended. One of the largest group of people who try to use discretion is those in politics. For obvious reasons, they want to win the election and get into office. For those of you who are familiar with the comedy of Jeff Dunham and Achmed his puppet, there was a Christmas special they did where Achmed stated "he didn't want to offend anybody. He wanted to be politically correct."

There have been many mistakes regarding discretion with people in the public limelight, but we all know we have had our own slip-ups in private. Solomon is saying that discretion will keep us in good condition, safe from harm or loss and prevent decay. Who wouldn't want that?

Chapter Three

Proverbs 3:3

"Let not mercy and truth forsake thee: bind them about thy neck; write them upon the table of thine heart."

Truth and mercy are necessary ingredients of wisdom. "Ye have heard that it hath been said, an eye for an eye, and a tooth for a tooth: But I say unto you, that ye resist not evil: but whosoever shall smite thee on thy right cheek, turn to him the other also. And if any man will sue thee at the law, and take away thy coat, let him have thy cloak also. And whosoever shall compel thee to go a mile, go with him twain. Give to him that asketh thee, and from him that would borrow of thee turn not thou away."–Matthew 5:38-42.

Og Mandino an American author who wrote the best seller "The Greatest Salesman in the World", which sold over 50 million copies and has been translated into over 25 different languages wrote the following quote. "I am here for a purpose and that purpose is to grow into a mountain, not to shrink to a grain of sand. Henceforth will I apply all my efforts to become the highest mountain of all and I will strain my potential until it cries for mercy."

Elizabeth Cady Stanton a writer and a women's' rights activist had the following quote. "Truth is the only safe ground to stand on."

Now we can see how important mercy and truth are. They are so critical to our walk with God that we are to keep them close to us via our neck and heart.

Proverbs 3:5

"Trust in the Lord with all thine heart and lean not unto thine own understanding."

How many of us know God knows much more than we do? With that in mind, God knows what direction to steer us to prevent pitfalls because he is Jehovah Jirah.

As human beings, we change our mind so often that we cannot trust ourselves. One minute we want Olive Garden for dinner then we decide later we want Chinese takeout. Oliver Herford was an American writer, artist, and illustrator who was quoted as saying, "A woman's mind is cleaner than a man's: she changes it more often."

I wrote in one of my blogs titled "Rollercoasters" why is it we climb into a rollercoaster giddy, sweaty, pumped with adrenaline and faith that the ride will be awesome? We never have wavering faith that our feet will never land safely on the ground within 3 ½ to 4 minutes after the ride's inception? So, if we are so confident and stable and grounded in our faith in a manmade steel object why is our faith so flimsy in our creator? We need to trust God every second of every day.

Proverbs 3:6

"In all thy ways acknowledge him, and he shall direct thy paths."

Acknowledging the Lord is admitting He is infinitely wise. He knows how to handle every circumstance you come across. We all will face predicaments, sometimes arduous, every day of our lives, however, you need to Let Go and Let God.

To acknowledge God means to place a high priority on him. We need to keep him first in all things. We need to think about him, pray to him, look to him, read about him, surround ourselves around people who do the same, and above all praise him.

How do we accomplish these things? Before our feet hit the floor in the mornings, afternoons, or evenings depending on your schedule and when your day starts you thank him for life. The next day is not promised to us so we must be grateful. We need to pray to him throughout the day. We need to pick up our bible and dust it off and read it. Sure, tablets and cell phones and other devices are great, but the actual bible book was the original. Yes, we need to go to church and be around like-minded people. Now I already know what some of you will say. There are more sinners in the church than anywhere else. Guess what where the sinners are is where God will be. Stop making excuses just go! Praise God for all that he has done in your life. Remember, he doesn't owe you anything. He already sent his son Jesus Christ to die on the cross for you.

Proverbs 3:9

"Honour the Lord with thy substance, and with the firstfruits of all thine increase."

Just because this is the 21st century God has not changed his mind. We are to still honor him with the first portion of our earnings the tithe. We get a clear picture of this in Malachi 3:8-12.

"Will a man rob God? Yet ye have robbed me. But ye say, wherein have we robbed thee? In tithes and offerings. Ye are cursed with a curse: for ye have robbed me, even this whole nation. Bring ye all the tithes into the storehouse, that there may be meat in mine house, and prove me now herewith, saith the Lord of hosts, if I will not open you the windows of heaven, and pour you out a blessing, that there shall not be room enough to receive it. And I will rebuke the devourer for your sakes, and he shall not destroy the fruits of your ground; neither shall your vine cast her fruit before the time in the field, saith the Lord of hosts. And all nations shall call you blessed: for ye shall be a delightsome land, saith the Lord of hosts."–Malachi 3:8-12.

As I mentioned in the previous proverb God doesn't owe us anything, but he says in Malachi I will rebuke the devour for your sakes, and he shall not destroy the fruits of your ground. Really how much clearer can it be?

Proverbs 3:16

"Length of days is in her right hand; and in her left-hand riches and honour."

Solomon explains in this proverb that we can have the opportunity to live a long life on the one hand and be blessed with riches and honor if we will seek God first on the other hand. King Solomon imparted superior financial insight in proverbs.

It is vitally important that we allow God to take the lead role in all aspects of our lives so then we can live a tranquil life because we know he is in control and only wants the best for us. When we can be at peace, that means we have no stress in our lives. Stress kills. They say anger weakens the liver, grief weakens the lungs, worry weakens the stomach, stress weakens the heart and brain and fear fails the kidneys. If we leave everything to God, then we don't have to worry about these things disrupting our bodies.

Solomon taught excellent economic wisdom in his proverbs. "He becometh poor that dealeth with a slack hand: but the hand of the diligent maketh rich."–Proverbs 10:4. "Whoso keepeth the fig tree shall eat the fruit thereof: so, he that waiteth on his master shall be honoured."–Proverbs 27:18.

Seeking wisdom will allow us to live a life of integrity as far as God is concerned and then God will grant us an illustrious life before people. "But seek ye first the kingdom of God, and his righteousness; and all these things shall be added unto you."–Matthew 6:33. The honor that we seek should be honor conferred by God.

Proverbs 3:27

"Withhold not good from them to whom it is due when it is in the power of thine hand to do it."

When we see a need and we can assist someone we should do so. If we can afford it, we should be a blessing to others. Jesus said, "For ye have the poor always with you; but me ye have not always."–Matthew 26:11.

Then there is the other side of the coin. It is important how we deal with people when we owe money to them. When we owe people debts, we need to do all we have to, so they are repaid what we owe them.

This is the reason the daytime court shows will always be there. People expect to just ask, beg, plead, or demand you assist them however when the noose is off their neck, they suddenly have amnesia. "Render therefore to all their dues: tribute to whom tribute is due; custom to whom custom; fear to whom fear; honour to whom honour. Owe no man anything, but to love one another: for he that loveth another hath fulfilled the law."–Romans 13:7-8.

Chapter Four

Proverbs 4:5

"Get wisdom, get understanding; forget it not; neither decline from the words of my mouth."

How do you go about obtaining wisdom? Getting wisdom means you must have a strong desire for it. There are 86,400 seconds in a day. Have you spent any of them working to get wisdom and understanding? If your quest is to get wisdom, then it is vital you spend time with wise people. "Looking unto Jesus the author and finisher of our faith; who for the joy that was set before him endured the cross, despising the shame, and is set down at the right hand of the throne of God."–Hebrews 12:2.

One of the best outlets for you to gain wisdom is reading the Book of Proverbs. It has been designed easily for you to do that since all you need to do is read one chapter in the book daily.

An acquisition is the learning or developing of a skill, habit, or quality. In, this proverb, Solomon the son of David who was the king of Israel is saying that it's of great importance that wisdom and understanding are the most vital acquisitions you can ever gain. A visual example of two things going hand in hand like this would be hot apple pie and vanilla ice cream.

Proverbs 4:6

"Forsake her not, and she shall preserve thee: love her, and she shall keep thee."

If you enlist wisdom, it will protect you from great suffering and emotional distress. Since French is one language of love, we will call her Dame Wisdom. This proverb speaks as if it is a love story. The father tells his son not to forsake her which means not to abandon her.

Every time we go out on our own and leave wisdom behind, we are abandoning her. Then when things don't work out, we return to her battered and beaten with scars. If only we had not forsaken our love Wisdom.

Every day we make choices that can either benefit us or cause consequences. If daily, we would just listen to Dame Wisdom and follow what she says then she will protect us from evil and foolishness.

God has offered us a special guide to assist us daily which is Dame Wisdom. We can compare wisdom in this verse to man's best friend. Man's best friend is a common phrase about dogs referring to their close relations, loyalty, and companionship with their owners. Get close to wisdom just like how you would cuddle up with your dog if you have one. Now if you have a cat or a bird, the principal is still the same.

Proverbs 4:7

"Wisdom is the principal thing; therefore, get wisdom: and with all thy getting get understanding."

Wisdom is the principal thing. Wisdom is the basis for living a fulfilled life. Wisdom will lift you up. Wisdom will bless your life. When we embrace wisdom, we pull it close to us like our spouse.

It is important to grasp the power of understanding. When we are lacking in understanding we are ensnared without difficulty. Understanding means to get a mental grasp to comprehend something.

If you own a car, you realize it must have a battery in it. The battery has a positive and negative post. If you ever need to boost your car, you understand that the battery cables are red and black, and you must place the cables in the proper position to charge the battery. In life understanding is so critical that is why it goes hand in hand with wisdom.

Proverbs 4:8

"Exalt her, and she shall promote thee: she shall bring thee to honour, when thou dost embrace her."

Exalt and embrace wisdom, and the Lord and people will promote and honor you. When you exalt something, you hold it in very high regard. This is the way wisdom and understanding are to be treated. They must have a premium placed upon them.

Wisdom will prevent you from possibly making disastrous mistakes in your life that could be very costly like texting and driving and you wind up killing a person.

Understanding will cause you to have forgiveness which is what Jesus wants us to do as he did which is what he said when he was nailed to the cross. "Then said Jesus, Father, forgive them; for they know not what they do. And they parted his raiment and cast lots." - Luke 23:34.

Proverbs 4:13

"Take fast hold of instruction; let her not go: keep her; for she is thy life."

It is critical for us to realize that instruction is a driving force in our lives. We need to realize that if we love and follow instructions, they will benefit us and if we don't, they can destroy us.

For those of us who drive we remember when we went to take our road test if we didn't follow what the driving instructor said we would not have passed and received our license. From the time we first got behind the wheel with our brand-new shiny driver's license, we knew there were driving rules to follow which still apply today. Green means go, yellow means yield, and red means stop. If we reverse any of those there could be dangerous repercussions from that.

Now for those of you who don't drive here is another angle. Say you enjoy working with your hands and this could be for you or your children. You purchase an airplane or helicopter that works with a remote you must assemble. If you don't follow the instructions that come in the package you can never put the object together correct and it will never fly and there is no enjoyment. So how important is instruction? Just like the verse says, "she is thy life."

Proverbs 4:24

"Put away from thee a froward mouth, and perverse lips put far from thee."

"O generation of vipers, how can ye, being evil, speak good things? for out of the abundance of the heart the mouth speaketh."–Matthew 12:34.

Today's society is growing more and more raucous every day. Vulgar and nasty language is now a regular daily thing. Control your speech and contain your tongue. "Even a fool, when he holdeth his peace, is counted wise: and he that shutteth his lips is esteemed a man of understanding."–Proverbs 17:28. "A wholesome tongue is a tree of life: but perverseness therein is a breach in the spirit."–Proverbs 15:4. "Let no corrupt communication proceed out of your mouth, but that which is good to the use of edifying, that it may minister grace unto the hearers."–Ephesians 4:29. A vulgar mouth will damage your reputation.

I know he has taken a tremendous downward spiral in recent years but at one point he was the King of Comedy. I am referring to none other than Bill Cosby. What made him so great is that he could make you laugh with tears running down your face and if you weren't careful and a bathroom was not close by, you might have an accident. He was not only the king of comedy; he was the king of clean non-vulgar comedy. Who says to get your point across you must use curse words? Try it sometime not just because the bible says not to have a froward mouth and perverse lips but just to see the expression of someone's face when you tell them what you think, which way to go, and how to get there with sophisticated words that will leave them scratching their head with a quizzical look on their face and reaching for the first dictionary they can find.

Chapter Five

Proverbs 5:18

"Let thy fountain be blessed: and rejoice with the wife of thy youth."

This proverb encourages us to rejoice in the wife of our youth. Wedded men have a fountain. Men should express gratitude to God for their wives and the fountain that God has blessed them with by guarding it, giving recognition to it, and favoring it. It tells us that to enjoy physical intimacy with our wife is to allow our fountain to be blessed. In the entire book, the Song of Solomon God speaks about the joys of physical intimacy within marriage. Adultery ruins this bountiful thing.

When something is blessed, it is made holy or consecrated. When you undergo consecration, this means the separation of oneself from things that are unclean especially anything that would contaminate one's relationship with God or a spouse.

Why is it when something is shiny, new, and bright it is spellbinding but as soon as it ages it is no longer desired? If you have ever purchased a brand-new car, the feeling is exhilarating. The new paint job, the brand-new tires, the new car smell, it's all good. However, after some wear and tear the new car smell is gone unless you buy car fresheners. The paint job gets dull. The tires don't have enough tread and then you think about trading it in for a newer model. Yes, you can do that, and people do it every day, but a car isn't consecrated like marriage is! Whether you have a huge elaborate wedding, or you go to city hall and the ceremony goes by so quickly where you feel you were just auctioned off the same principle applies.

The words have not changed from to have and to hold, from this day forward, for better for worse, for richer for poorer, in sickness and in health, until death do us part. Today society makes divorce so easy that with the slightest amount of friction in a marriage one party is ready to abandon ship and give up. There is a saying that the grass is not always greener on the other side. How would you feel when it is your time to leave this life and you are standing at the pearly gates and God says, "I gave up on you a long time ago. Take the elevator down to the bottom floor and enjoy Hell!"

Proverbs 5:19

"Let her be as the loving hind and pleasant roe; let her breasts satisfy thee at all times; and be thou ravished always with her love."

Throughout Proverbs Chapter 5 Solomon is warning his son about the perils of adultery. Solomon is talking to his son about how important the choices are that we make in life. Solomon is advising his son about three important choices. He needs to cherish his spouse, value her body and sexuality, and solely permit only her fondness and devotion to devour him.

A hind is a female deer that is known for their grace, speed, lustrous eyes and human strength and beauty. A gazelle is noted for their graceful movements and lustrous eyes.

Ladies we all know when a man has an interest in us our breasts and buttocks are normally something, they take notice of. We are also aware that their eyes never leave us especially on a first or second date. They are consumed with looking at us. Men, how is it that when you were in the dating stage everything was great but as soon as you have been married for a while the all-consuming fire you had for your wife has burned out? Remember when you step outside the bounds of marriage and engage in adultery it's like going to a buffet. You never know what you can get. You could pick up and STD, syphilis, gonorrhea, herpes, or just place your order early to be delivered six feet under because you contacted aids. Is it worth it? Is it because she has put on a little weight or is it that certain parts don't stand up as high as they used to? That goes both ways. Remember what the bible says, "What therefore God hath joined together, let not man put asunder."–Mark 10:9.

Proverbs 5:20

"And why wilt thou, my son, be ravished with a strange woman, and embrace the bosom of a stranger?"

The way you stay away from craving another woman other than your spouse is to keep a noble marriage with your spouse. Bitterness and reflecting on faults will harm your fondness for your spouse. This is how adultery winds up at your doorstep. "Husbands, love your wives, and be not bitter against them."–Colossians 3:19.

In the state of Florida down in the Miami area it blesses us to have a consummate entertainer. He is called Pit Bull and known as Mr. Worldwide. Accompanied by Yandel and Chacal they released a song called "Ay Mi Dios." In that song, he states, "The grass always looks green on the other side till you get to the other side."

This is the mistake that is made by married couples who commit adultery. I remember early in my marriage I said to my husband when we went out car shopping, "I like this one. I like the way it looks." He told me then and has reiterated it several times through the years, "Don't go by the look!"

When a male or female goes outside the boundaries of their marriage, it is always because of the look. You don't get to know how a person thinks, what's deep in their heart, what dreams and aspirations they have, their idiosyncrasies, or anything else until you get to know them. To get to know them you must spend time with them and have conversations with them.

Adultery doesn't care whether you are an Ivey leaguer and how intelligent you are. It is only about quenching a raging fire that is all-consuming. Adultery is sometimes only a one-night stand which can prove just as costly as a long-standing affair.

Last year for Christmas I went to purchase a ring for my husband at IDC and was told by the salesman that a lot of their volume comes from married men that not only have girlfriends, but some have mistresses too. Either way, it's costly. It will hit you in your pocket with all the gifts you must purchase, or it can take your life if you get a sexually transmitted disease. The choice is yours but no matter what God does not approve of it.

26

Chapter Six

Proverbs 6:9

"How long wilt thou sleep, O sluggard? when wilt thou arise out of thy sleep?"

Sleep is vital for every person. If you disagree see how you feel and how your body operates when you have not had any sleep for several days. However, it can become a dangerous thing if you indulge in it too much to where you refuse to work or do anything.

For things to change you must change. Success never happens by accident. A person must work hard to become successful. You must have a game plan. It must discipline you. You must have dreams and goals.

As a writer, it is easy to become complacent and say, "oh I'll do, research and writing another day when I'm in the mood." Then the next thing you know the days have turned into weeks, months, sometimes years and then you look back and say, "where did the time go?" Believe it or not, it's even harder to regroup once you have lost focus like that for so long by becoming a sluggard.

Life is short. We were all created by God to fulfill a purpose in life to be a laborer and not a sluggard where your purpose never blossoms and shines bright and you carry it to your grave.

Proverbs 6:17-19

"A proud look, a lying tongue, and hands that shed innocent blood."

What is an abomination? It is a thing that causes disgust or hatred. In, the next three verses we see there are things that the Lord hates. First a proud look. We are all created equal, so it makes no sense to be proud or haughty. Pride puts itself equal to, or above the Lord. Pride tells God I don't need you. I can handle it myself. "Pride will always be the longest distance between people. For pride is spiritual cancer; it eats up the very possibility of love or contentment, or even common sense."–C.S. Lewis. "Pride must die in you, or nothing of heaven can live in you."–Andrew Murray.

"Pride is concerned with whom is right. Humility is concerned with what is right."–Ezra Taft Benson. Making mistakes is better than faking perfections. Satan fell from heaven because of pride. There is an old saying, "Tell the truth and shame the Devil." According to social psychologist Aldert Vrij of the University of Portsmouth in England "lying is more cognitively demanding than telling the truth." If lying is more demanding on the brain and God said he hates it, then just don't do it and tell the truth. When you tell the truth, someone can ask you the same question ten days or even ten years from now and they will receive the same answer from you. Hmm.... Men take that as a warning since

28

women have long memories and are prone to ask the same question more than once.

This last one really requires no explanation. It is one of the Ten Commandments number six. "Thou shalt not kill." You can locate it in the book of Exodus chapter 20. So, if it's one of the Ten Commandments you think God was serious?

Proverbs 6:18

"An heart that deviseth wicked imaginations, feet that be swift in running to mischief."

The Lord despises it when a person is always concocting ways to get into trouble. That person has evil intentions in their minds all the time. They are quick to do mischief and show no regard for sin's negative calling.

Everybody knows the famous cartoon "Tom and Jerry." Tom is a cat who is constantly planning ways to capture and kill Jerry the mouse. Tom, however, is rarely victorious in capturing Jerry because of his intelligent cunning ways. However, that has never stopped Tom from using drastic measures to trap Jerry such as hammers, explosives, axes, firecrackers, firearms, and even traps with poison in them.

This example is a cartoon but unfortunately, people are doing this to each other every day. God is not pleased when we live our lives in this fashion.

Proverbs 6:19

"A false witness that speaketh lies, and he that soweth discord among brethren."

God hates liars. A person who lies has no regard for the truth. It grieves God when there is a lack of harmony between people and constant disagreement. "Blessed are the peacemakers: for they shall be called the children of God."–Matthew 5:9.

Some people love to cause discord and distress between people and after they do their devilment, they go off to the sidelines to see their handiwork and smirk. I believe if everyone who lied had the same fate as Pinocchio lying would cease quickly. For those of you who don't know the story of Pinocchio, he had a very short nose and every time he lied it grew longer so that way everyone knew he was lying.

Proverbs 6:23

"For the commandment is a lamp, and the law is light, and reproofs of instruction are the way of life."

God gave us the Ten Commandments to be a lamp for us. A lamp has several definitions one being a celestial body.

When God created the earth, he created lights, "And God made two great lights; the greater light to rule the day, and the lesser light to rule the night: he made the stars also." Genesis 1:16. When you go out with your car at night, you turn on your headlights, so you can see where you are going. That light shows you what's ahead and what direction to travel. The same applies here where the word says, "the law is the light."

What God says in his word guides us and take us safely on our course of life. If we can trust the headlights on our vehicles, why can't we trust the laws of God? In, God's instruction and correction is life. Do you choose to live with the light or perish with the darkness?

Proverbs 6:32

"But whoso committeth adultery with a woman lacketh understanding: he that doeth it destroyeth his own soul."

God has blessed us all with intelligence. Wisdom however we must pray and ask for as Solomon did.

There are things out there that will destroy your soul and adultery is one. A person who allows themselves to get caught up in this lack understanding they have no heart.

At Christmastime especially, there are so many commercials of animal shelters asking you to adopt. The pictures of the dogs and cats just melt your heart. Where is that same heart when you go outside of the boundaries of your marriage?

Book of Proverbs

Chapter Seven

Proverbs 7:2

"Keep my commandments, and live, and my law as the apple of thine eye."

God expects us to listen and take him serious with everything else he says besides the commandments. An excellent example of this is the story of Lot and his wife.

God destroyed the city of Sodom because of the vast wickedness that the people of Sodom were doing. Two angels visited Lot and urged him at dawn to get his family and flee Sodom, so they would not be part of the impending disaster for the iniquity of the city. The angels advised Lot to flee for your life and don't look back or else it will destroy you. Unfortunately, Lot's wife didn't listen and turned back to look at the burning city and became a pillar of salt, while Lot and his two daughters kept running.

God allowed us to crucify his son Jesus Christ on the cross for all our sins. "For God so loved the world, that he gave his only begotten Son, that whosoever believeth in him should not perish, but have everlasting life."–John 3:16.

We all are the apple of God's eye. He is fond and proud of us all.

Proverbs 7:26-27

"For she hath cast down many wounded: yea, many strong men have been slain by her. Her house is the way to hell, going down to the chambers of death."

In the bible, there is the story of Samson and Delilah. Samson was a Nazirite who had great strength who was in love with Delilah. The name of Delilah is a Hebrew name and in Arabic, Delilah means faithless one. That would explain why when Delilah was bribed by the lords of the Philistines to uncover the source of Samson's strength she did so willingly.

Once she could get Samson to tell her where the source of his strength came from which was his hair, she had it cut off while he was sleeping and then turned him over to the Philistines. The story says the Philistines gauged his eyes and Samson became blind. Samson called unto the Lord and asked him to strengthen him one more time, so he could avenge the Philistines for destroying his sight. The Lord obliged Samson, and he destroyed the Philistines even though he died along with them.

Men be careful of beautiful seductive women because they are very beguiling and ultimately it can cost you your life.

Chapter Eight

Proverbs 8:10-11

"Receive my instruction, and not silver; and knowledge rather than choice gold. For wisdom is better than rubies, and all the things that may be desired are not to be compared to it."

Instruction and knowledge surround every one of us daily. If we are just starting a new job, they instruct us on how to perform the work. If we are a seasoned employee, then we will provide knowledge about the work. All of us at one time or another have had to go to the doctor because we were not feeling well. When the doctor gives you that prescription you give it to the pharmacist who then dispenses your medication to you and all medications always have instructions and knowledge. The instructions advise you on how to take the medicine and then there is also the knowledge that tells you what side effects you can have.

That old saying that diamonds are a girl best friend is true but silver, gold, and rubies my birthstone are also nice. However as precious as these stones maybe they don't compare to instruction, knowledge, and wisdom. I realize I may give away my age here but back in 1984, there was a very successful show called "Lifestyles of the Rich and Famous" that played on TV until 1995.

It was great to get a peek into the lives of the wealthy and see the places they traveled to. It helped you to dream. Dreaming and imagining are great. Albert Einstein said it best, "Imagination is Everything. It is the preview of life's coming attractions." However, if we look at the example I used above, and you take more or less medication than it instructs you could wind up in the hospital or maybe something worst. Instruction and knowledge are important.

Proverbs 8:13

"The fear of the Lord is to hate evil: pride, and arrogancy, and the evil way, and the froward mouth, do I hate."

Let's look at this down to its most adolescence form. Santa Claus vs The Grinch. Santa Claus always asks kids if they have been naughty or nice. The Grinch we know is always naughty. Not every day is the same. Some days we feel great and others we feel blah. Jesus died for us on the cross for all our sins however that does not mean we can just go buck wild and sin constantly on purpose. We should strive to emulate Jesus constantly. Sure, there are days where we may fall short and Jesus knows of that and loves us unconditionally, anyway. We should try to follow the Golden Rule, "Do unto others as you would have them do unto you." We all know people who are evil in their ways, arrogant, prideful, and who cannot speak one sentence without using a dirty word. We should strive to be nice and joyful. Instead of being arrogant be humble. We should try to speak respectfully to people the same way we would want to be spoken to. We all can change it's just a matter of how badly you want to.

Proverbs 8:18-19

"Riches and honour are with me; yea, durable riches, and righteousness. My fruit is better than gold, yea, than fine gold; and my revenue than choice silver."

Let me remind you all that I am using the King James Bible for all Bible verses. The most important word here is durable. The meaning of the word says to exist for a long time without significant deterioration in quality or value. All homeowners want the roof on their house to be durable. Married couples want their marriage to be durable. Most people want to be working for a durable company, so they can keep having a steady paycheck. All material things no matter what they get to a point where they are not durable anymore. In verse 18 God expands by using the words fruit and revenue. God is advising us that all his riches are durable, solid, safe and honorable and we should be more inclined to chase after what he offers than earthly things.

Proverbs 8:21

"That I may cause those that love me to inherit substance; and I will fill their treasures."

Do you ever wonder to yourself how sometimes a friend, co-worker, family member, are always doing the things you want to do? They always seem to be able to take a vacation every year. Every three years they seem to get a new car. You have an intimate enough relationship with them you know what their financial situation is, and they earn less than you so how is this happening?

They are blessed. They have the favor of God surrounding them. They love God and so he is increasing their substance and earthly treasures. Even when things are strained trust, God. Keep a smile on your face, keep a good attitude, keep tithing, keep helping others. This may be things that these people you know are doing and that is why they are blessed despite their finances. My grandmother used to tell me, "as long as you have manners and respect you can go around this entire world without a penny in your pocket."

Proverbs 8:34-36

"Blessed is the man that heareth me, watching daily at my gates, waiting at the posts of my doors. For whoso findeth me findeth life and shall obtain favour of the Lord. But he that sinneth against me wrongeth his own soul: all they that hate me love death."

It has prompted all of us at one time or another to do something. Maybe we were reminded of something we should do. This is the Holy Spirit. We should all be ready and receptive to listen and follow through with what the Holy Spirit says. The third part of the Trinity the Holy Spirit is always with us because he lives within us. The minute we receive Christ the Holy Spirit comes to live within us. "Know ye not that ye are the temple of God, and that the Spirit of God dwelleth in you?."–1 Corinthians 3:16. We should all be attentive and listening out for the voice of God when he speaks to us via the Holy Spirit and acting on what he says. We should search for God, craving an intimate relationship with God and not going against his will because it means devastation for us.

I spoke about the voice in my first book "Miracles of Direction Miracles of Conquest Miracles of Provision Miracles of Purpose." I have a personal account of going to the supermarket. I live close to three supermarkets and I have my favorite but this day I heard the voice say go to a different one. As always in life we have choices. I listened and obeyed and was rewarded with an unadvertised sale of Bumble Bee tuna on sale. This is the only tuna my family eats, and so it was a great blessing to us.

Book of Proverbs

Chapter Nine

Proverbs 9:6

"Forsake the foolish, and live, and go in the way of understanding."

If you want to live, give up your foolishness and let understanding guide your steps. Leave your simple ways behind and live; learn to use good judgment.

At one point or another as a youngster, we had all done something foolish. In, a lot of cases it may have been done just because of peer pressure. Possibly high adrenaline moves like car-surfing, simple practical jokes on people, experimenting with substances, writing graffiti or many others. However, as you grow older wisdom should keep you clear of foolish moves. Recently a man I know wanted to give his girlfriend a great few days celebrating her birthday. He made a reservation at a charming hotel and intended to show her an exciting time. He thought he could just have a wonderful time for the few days and then do a charge-back on his credit card regarding the hotel and get his money back. He issued the charge-back and the credit card company deposited the funds back onto his card. What he didn't expect is that an investigation would be done and after they completed it when he least expected it all his funds regarding the hotel expense were withdrawn from his credit card and that left him overdrawn and despondent. As we grow older, we should give up foolishness and have the maturity of mind.

Proverbs 9:9-11

"Give instruction to a wise man, and he will be yet wiser: teach a just man, and he will increase in learning. The fear of the Lord is the beginning of wisdom: and the knowledge of the holy is understanding. For by me thy days shall be multiplied, and the years of thy life shall be increased."

A wise person never reaches the point in life where he cannot increase in wisdom. He never becomes obstinate or unruly. A wise person is continually looking to be a suction. Almost all of us have a device in the home we use as a suction. If you have a carpet in your home, you have a vacuum cleaner to pick up dirt, etc. If you have straws in your home, you use them to drink your beverages. Point of info the state of Washington mainly the city of Seattle has now banned the use of plastic straws to reduce marine pollution. Beware this trend could take effect everywhere, eventually.

Wise people are teachable because they are humble and exhibit a fear of the Lord. There is an animal called the honey badger that is the most fearless of all animals however they are afraid of mongooses. Those of you that have dogs some of them are afraid of thunder and lightning and scurry away most times under the bed when they hear the sounds. When I was a little girl, we had a Norwegian Elkhound dog, and we named him Thunder because the day we purchased him from the pet shop it was thundering and lightning. It became the most hilarious thing every time it thundered that he went diving under the bed afraid of the thunder. A dog's hearing has a far wider range of sound frequencies than humans.

Stated in verse 11 if we have wisdom and understanding it will grant us long life. In the bible when God changed his name from Abram to Abraham God said they would know him as the father of many nations. They called Abraham the father of biblical faith. Because of his faith, Abraham lived to be 175 years old. Since the death of 117-year-old Chiyo Miyako of Japan on 22 July 2018, 118-year-old Kane Tanaka, also of Japan, born 2 January 1903, is the oldest living person in the world whose age has been documented. Closer to home "The First Lady of Television" Betty White 99 years old has stated she has no plans to retire. "I intend to be in the saddle forever." Betty White has a deep faith along with wisdom and understanding that is why she is living proof of Proverbs 9:11.

Book of Proverbs

Chapter Ten

Proverbs Chapter 10:2

"Treasures of wickedness profit nothing: but righteousness delivereth from death."

Most of if not all of us have heard the saying "what's done in the dark will come into the light". That statement continues to ring true day after day. My husband loves to watch the TV show Forensic Files which aired from 1996 to 2011. Time and time again you would see spouses that committed murder just to get life insurance money payouts. Eventually, they were caught and placed in jail for their heinous act. They now have a Forensic Files II that debuted in 2020. There is also another show called "I almost got away with it" which aired from 2010 to 2016. This show told the true stories of people who had committed crimes and had avoided arrest or capture but ultimately ended up being caught.

Many of us know people that chose what they thought was the more glamorous life of selling drugs and ultimately sometimes when a deal went wrong committing murder. However, most of these people are dead, in jail, or recovering drug addicts now. This lifestyle benefited none of them because the exorbitant amount of money ruined their lives; issues with family and friends became explosive; and turbulent living, and they exhausted the money like water. Money makes an excellent servant, but a poor master.

Proverbs Chapter 10:3

"The Lord will not suffer the soul of the righteous to famish: but he casteth away the substance of the wicked."

"And whatsoever we ask, we receive of him, because we keep his commandments, and do those things that are pleasing in his sight."–1 John 3:22. Solomon is telling us that the wicked are not living lives that are pleasing to God therefore, they cannot come to God in confidence.

Cain committed the first murder in the bible by stoning his brother Abel. God had asked Cain and Abel to bring sacrifices to him from their produce and God preferred Abel's and apparently, jealousy rose up in him and so he killed Abel. Ironically, later in life, Cain died because the stones on the home he built gave away and the house fell on him and the stones killed him.

Now with this example, we don't have to go that far back in history. Only back to November 19, 2017, when the cult leader Charles Manson died. After forming the Manson family, a quasi-commune in California and the deaths of numerous people they sentenced him to serve out his life in a California state prison. He died of cardiac arrest, respiratory failure, and colon cancer. When you live by the sword, you die by the sword.

Proverbs Chapter 10:4

"He becometh poor that dealeth with a slack hand: but the hand of the diligent maketh rich."

There is wisdom in learning the value of hard work. It pays off in life in the long run. How many times have you heard somebody won the lottery and five years later they are broke? When you work hard to get something you appreciate and care for it better than something that is just handed to you.

There is another TV show that my husband loves to watch called "Swamp People". I am not an alligator person, so I only see it when I am in the kitchen and he is watching it. I will say one thing if these people didn't live in the bayou and were city people and into corporate America, they would be exceedingly rich. Not just millionaires but billionaires. Their drive, persistence, never give up attitude, work ethic to fill all their tags for alligators they must catch in the one-month season is tremendous. They believe in hard work, dedication, and will endure the long hours if it takes their last breath. If you want to get ahead in life, don't expect God to do it all for you. You have a part, and he has a part. If you do your part, he will do his!

Proverbs Chapter 10:6

"Blessings are upon the head of the just: but violence covereth the mouth of the wicked."

In this verse, Solomon speaks about the blessings the righteous receive versus the distress and disturbances the wicked evil people experience because of the words they speak.

Most people are literally not aware of how important the words they speak are. If more people were cognizant how important their words are, they probably would not say the things they say. No person can really determine what happens in your life, but you and God's words are more important in your life than your own words. How you feel deep in your heart comes out through your mouth. The earth you plant seeds into is like how your heart is a receptacle for the seeds you put into it. When you plant seeds of corn, it is impossible for you to reap a harvest of collard greens.

Why don't you try testing this out for yourself? This example is not specifically for you but let's say you always say, "no matter what I always get caught in traffic." You also say this often, "I am so fortunate that I never get stuck in a line with a person with a lot of coupons when I go grocery shopping." Watch the words you speak for a week and see what areas you are blessed and what areas things are difficult for you and adjust accordingly.

Proverbs Chapter 10:12

"Hatred stirreth up strifes: but love covereth all sins."

"But if ye forgive not men their trespasses, neither will your Father forgive your trespasses."–Matthew 6:15

"And be ye kind one to another, tenderhearted, forgiving one another, even as God for Christ's sake hath forgiven you."–Ephesians 4:32

"But I say unto you which hear, love your enemies, do good to them which hate you."–Luke 6:27

"Judge not, and ye shall not be judged: condemn not, and ye shall not be condemned: forgive, and ye shall be forgiven."–Luke 6:37.

All of us have things about us that are challenging, and this is one of mines. I have always had a difficult time forgiving people that have hurt me but, I remember Philippians 1:6 "Being confident of this very thing, that he which hath begun a good work in you will perform it until the day of Jesus Christ." Every time I remember that I know that God is working on changing me and I have seen improvements. I have been learning not to acknowledge "an eye for an eye, and a tooth for a tooth." For example, just because someone cut you off in traffic that does not mean you step on the gas catch us to them and then cut them off. First, that could cause an accident if you cut them too close and they can't step on the gas fast enough or worse in today's society they get mad and catch up to you and roll down their window and shoot. It's just not worth it! Remember God gives us beauty for ashes and double for our trouble. Do it like me do it one day at a time and take one step at a time.

Proverbs Chapter 10:15

"The rich man's wealth is his strong city: the destruction of the poor is their poverty."

If you are blessed to be wealthy, don't allow it to go to your head and take on a snobbish attitude and become prideful where you believe you are better than someone who doesn't have a bank account with lots of zeros behind the initial number.

Also, if you happen to be struggling and live from check to check or must get help don't make two mistakes. First, don't despise those who have more because you don't know how they gained their wealth and secondly don't believe where you are is where you will always be. Things will get better. Have faith and believe.

As a child of God, we should be judicious regarding our finances. Not using wisdom in our finances can cause great harm to us. Being ignorant of the fact that if you have money, you should be a blessing to others can also cause damage. "Thou shalt surely give him, and thine heart shall not be grieved when thou givest unto him: because that for this thing the Lord thy God shall bless thee in all thy works, and in all that thou puttest thine hand unto."– Deuteronomy 15:10. When it comes to being benevolent and giving to charity, one person comes to mind: Oprah Winfrey. As she gives away God continues to bless her exceedingly and abundantly.

So, what does all this mean? It means you must maintain a healthy perspective concerning money. Money makes an excellent servant, but a poor master.

Proverbs Chapter 10:21

"The lips of the righteous feed many: but fools die for want of wisdom."

God expects us to speak words that adorn, improve, elevate, and influence others. This is not an ideal that is just confined to pastors or leaders. As a believer God wants you to be a blessing to others with your words and actions. It costs nothing to be kind to others. Every day you can find something nice to say to someone and give them a smile. Think of the days when you are having a tough time, and someone smiles at you or compliments you on something. It warms your heart so why not reciprocate that to others? Take for instance you are in the grocery line and the customer in front of you is giving the cashier a hard time. When the transaction is completed, and it's your turn how about finding something nice to compliment the cashier on to lift their spirit. If nothing else to say the two magic words when your transaction is completed "Thank you."

Foolish or wicked people add no value to their lives or others. They speak without thinking and have nothing good to say. A good example of this is the Christmas story "The Grinch Who Stole Christmas." There is a new film simply called "the Grinch" that was released back on November 9, 2018.

Build a legacy for yourself that is "this person always had something uplifting to say that blessed my life. They always had a smile on their face."

Proverbs Chapter 10:22

"The blessing of the Lord, it maketh rich, and he addeth no sorrow with it."

Having money is not the issue; the issue arises when we get caught and seduced by its lure that it can handle all of life's problems.

It has destroyed families because of money. It can happen. Some people take a quick way out by selling drugs, guns, etc. Some others work over 60 or more hours per week claiming they are working so hard for the benefit of their family but in reality, they rarely spend time with their family.

Families do not sit down as a group anymore to have dinner. Either the mother or father is missing because of working long hours. These people don't have a personal, intimate relationship with God. Money has become their God and working long hours and being invisible from the dinner table has become their way of life. This is especially true of Thanksgiving Day. Retail stores have skipped this day and gone straight to preparing for Christmas. The stores now open on Thanksgiving Day around 4 pm depending on the store so they can start what they call Black Friday shopping. This is heinous!

God wants you to be financially secure, but he wants you to do it his way. God is capable to meet your needs in every situation. Keep God first place. God is the main line, not a sideline. When your priorities are right, everything else falls into place.

Proverbs 10:25

"As the whirlwind passeth, so is the wicked no more: but the righteous is an everlasting foundation."

Every one of us faces trials in life. It is unrealistic to think we will live our lives without challenges, especially when Jesus encountered his while he was here on earth. However, the good news is this, "These things I have spoken unto you, that in me ye might have peace. In the world ye shall have tribulation: but be of good cheer; I have overcome the world."–John 16:33.

In this verse, Solomon is saying that the wicked will not prevail, but the righteous will be covered and protected.

In the book of Exodus chapter 12 in the Bible God has had enough of Pharaoh's evil and wicked ways and has killed all the first-born Egyptians and instructs Moses to advise the children of Israel to kill a lamb "And they shall take of the blood, and strike it on the two side posts and on the upper door post of the houses. For I will pass through the land of Egypt this night and will smite all the firstborn in the land of Egypt, both man and beast; and against all the gods of Egypt I will execute judgment: I am the Lord. And the blood shall be to you for a token upon the houses where ye are: and when I see the blood, I will pass over you, and the plague shall not be upon you to destroy you when I smite the land of Egypt." As you can see the Lord protected the righteous and showed they are an everlasting foundation.

Proverbs 10:27

"The fear of the Lord prolongeth days: but the years of the wicked shall be shortened."

God's instruction, when put into practice, will add duration and character to our lives. When we pursue God and we acquire, accept his word, and apply knowledge, we will experience the advantage of a powerful long life. If we refuse to recognize that God is omnipotent and fear him our lives will be cut short.

There are countless stories of people living past the age of 100. My grandmother lived to be 100 years old and received a letter of congratulations from Ronald Reagan who was in office.

There is so much talk about dementia and Alzheimer's that it is alarming. I have two family members that have been diagnosed with this disease. However, both are over 90 years old.

Hollywood is currently blessed with two actresses that still work that are 84 years old and 99 years old. Betty White will become 100 years old on January 17, 2022. I am referring to none other than Jane Fonda and Betty White. Fonda was raised atheist but turned to Christianity. I am sure you realize how remarkable it is to be that age and still working where you need to memorize lines in a script for a movie or TV show.

This is what Solomon was referring to in this verse. God recompenses us with a long life for persons that have faith, trust, and belief in him and fashion their lives according to his teachings.

Chapter Eleven

Proverbs 11:2

"When pride cometh, then cometh shame: but with the lowly is wisdom."

Humility - freedom from pride or arrogance: the quality or state of being humble

Pride - inordinate self-esteem, a reasonable or justifiable self-respect, delight or elation arising from some act, possession, or relationship.

Pride is a weapon of our enemy. As believers we are not to think more highly of ourselves, then we should. When you are a prideful person you always focus on yourself. We are to do like Psalm 121:1 says "I will lift up mine eyes unto the hills, from whence cometh my help." When we keep our eyes on God, then we cannot keep our eyes on ourselves and become prideful. It is like the old saying "you cannot have your cake and eat it too." It means "you cannot simultaneously keep your cake and eat it". Once the cake is eaten, it is gone. Matthew 6:24 says, "No man can serve two masters: for either he will hate the one and love the other; or else he will hold to the one and despise the other. Ye cannot serve God and mammon."

Being humble doesn't mean that you lack confidence. Being humble just means you realize that it is not all about you. Even Jesus humbled himself, "Then answered Jesus and said unto them, Verily, verily, I say unto you, The Son can do nothing of himself, but what he seeth the Father do: for what things soever he doeth, these also doeth the Son likewise."–John 5:19. Since God is a jealous God, it is better and wiser for you to humble yourself before he humbles you. "And whosoever shall exalt himself shall be abased, and he that shall humble himself shall be exalted."–Matthew 23:12.

Proverbs 11:13

"A talebearer revealeth secrets: but he that is of a faithful spirit concealeth the matter."

Are you a trustworthy person? Do you mock your friends or others? A wise person realizes that you cannot slander others and expect to keep a sound reputation. "Now the parable is this: The seed is the word of God."–Luke 8:11. The words we speak are seeds. Just like a farmer who plants seeds for a harvest the words we say are seeds we are planting. A wise person realizes that the seeds they say regarding others will come back to them. You know the old quote from Mahalia Jackson, "If you dig one ditch you better dig two cause the trap you set just may be for you."

If you are the type of person that can't wait until it's break time, lunchtime, girls' night out, sports Sunday with the guys to talk about other people in a detrimental way this proverb is all about you.

A wise person realizes that he has his own flaws, and it is only because of the grace of God that he is where he is now. When you realize that you have flaws just like everyone else then you are not so quick to be judgmental regarding others.

Proverbs 11:24

"There is that scattereth, and yet increaseth; and there is that withholdeth more than is meet, but it tendeth to poverty."

Is money your God or do you trust God to bless you financially and provide for your needs and desires? Do you give freely or are you tight-fisted with your funds?

Solomon was the richest man in the world. God ordained Solomon to be king and asked him "what shall I give thee?" Solomon answered, "Give therefore thy servant an understanding heart to judge thy people, that I may discern between good and bad: for who is able to judge this thy so great a people?" "And the speech pleased the Lord, that Solomon had asked this thing. And God said unto him, Because thou hast asked this thing, and hast not asked for thyself long life; neither hast asked riches for thyself, nor hast asked the life of thine enemies; but hast asked for thyself understanding to discern judgment; Behold, I have done according to thy words: lo, I have given thee a wise and an understanding heart; so that there was none like thee before thee, neither after thee shall any arise like unto thee. And I have also given thee that which thou hast not asked, both riches, and honour: so that there shall not be any among the kings like unto thee all thy days."– 1King 3:9-13.

Many years ago, I was part of a study group in my church that was discussing your gifts. They used the book "Discover Your God-Given Gifts" written by Don & Katie Fortune. This is a book that discusses the seven gifts. I recommend this book to everyone. It discusses the gifts that God has given you and how to apply them in your life. At the end of the book, there are tests for you to take and according to your scores, it will let you know what your gifts are. It is possible to have more than one gift. I happen to have more than one and one of the gifts is a giver. Now my husband likes to say if anyone wanted to start a business and their location was near us, they would become very successful because I love to give to everyone. I operate within my gifting from God. Now not every one of us has that gifting but we can learn. There are some of us that are just downright hoarders and never want to give anything. This is not what God expects of us. "Give, and it shall be given unto you; good measure, pressed down, and shaken together, and running over, shall men give into your bosom. For with the same measure that ye mete withal it shall be measured to you again."–Luke 6:38

It is amazing how with telethons, or unspeakable acts like The Stoneman Douglas High School Shooting in Florida, or the horrific tragedy of The Trinidad Family where an entire family was killed except the mother (wife) in a car crash in Delaware on July 6, 2018 returning from a family vacation for the July 4th weekend. This tragedy left a mother without her four daughters and husband. People can give easily then but what about normal times. If God can bless you, then you can be a blessing to others.

Proverbs 11:28

"He that trusteth in his riches shall fall; but the righteous shall flourish as a branch."

Where does your trust lie? Money is here today and gone tomorrow. One day your investment portfolio is bulging and the next it is sexy slim. One day you are living safely and securely in your home and the next day a hurricane comes through and obliterates it and your insurance isn't sufficient to replace it. One week the NYSE is soaring into space and the next week people and firms are taking huge losses. The only guarantee in life is God!

"And the cares of this world, and the deceitfulness of riches, and the lusts of other things entering in, choke the word, and it becometh unfruitful."–Mark 4:19. Here we have the wealthiest man in the world Solomon telling us not to be deceived by money and don't trust in it. God wants us to prosper but don't forget who gives you the ability to prosper. God grants you mobility to work and earn a living to make money. God gives you favor, grace, and blesses your life so you can enjoy your life but remember you can't take it with you when he calls you home. Nobody who has left this life has carried a home, car, boat, plane, etc. with them. Some may have requested to be buried with their money or jewelry but guess what the funeral home and who is left behind has the final say. You are surely out of luck if they cremate you!

Those who keep their trust solely in God will continually be blessed exceedingly and abundantly. Money makes an excellent servant, but a poor master. In your life, God must be the priority and King of Kings.

Chapter Twelve

Proverbs 12:2

"A good man obtaineth favour of the Lord: but a man of wicked devices will he condemn."

What is the difference between good people and wicked people? One clear-cut answer is that good people look to be a blessing to others while wicked people are always scheming to hurt or destroy people. "Now ye are the body of Christ, and members in particular."–1 Corinthians 12:27. We are all members of the body of Christ. We all have a part. Just like our human body, every part depends on another. "For the body is not one member, but many. If the foot shall say, Because I am not the hand, I am not of the body; is it therefore not of the body? And if the ear shall say, Because I am not the eye, I am not of the body; is it therefore not of the body? If the whole body were an eye, where were the hearing? If the whole were hearing, where were the smelling? But now hath God set the members every one of them in the body, as it hath pleased him. And if they were all one member, where were the body? But now are they many members, yet but one body. And the eye cannot say unto the hand, I have no need of thee: nor again the head to the feet, I have no need of you. Nay, much more those members of the body, which seem to be more feeble, are necessary: And those members of the body, which we think to be less honourable, upon these we bestow more abundant honour; and our uncomely parts have more abundant comeliness."–1 Corinthians 12:14-23.

God desires for all of us to work together and be good to one another. The same way God designed all the parts of the body to work together is the same way we as his children are to work together, love one another, and be gracious to all.

Proverbs 12:4

"A virtuous woman is a crown to her husband: but she that maketh ashamed is as rottenness in his bones."

A good name is more valuable than riches because it can't be bought with money. It must be earned moment by moment, day by day, decision by decision. A virtuous woman is a godly woman who fears God and seeks to honor him. She is a woman who wants to be a blessing to her husband and has a strong moral character that doesn't cause shame to her husband but instead makes him proud. Maintaining a good name doesn't mean that you are perfect, but when you make mistakes, you learn from them and do what you can to make things right.

Examples of virtuous women in the bible are Mary, Sarah, Ruth, Elizabeth, and Priscilla. These women added value to their husbands, children and their own lives. The virtuous wife becomes an everlasting well of power, strength, and encouragement. Our ex-First Lady Michelle LaVaughn Robinson Obama is a fantastic example of a modern-day virtuous woman.

Proverbs 12:14

"A man shall be satisfied with good by the fruit of his mouth: and the recompence of a man's hands shall be rendered unto him."

It is vital that when we open our mouths; we speak words of faith because we can do all things through Christ which strengthens us. Words are powerful! That is how God created the earth. Words are powerful, and we must think before we speak. Since we are so lackadaisical with our words that is why sometimes we have been hung by the tongue. "But I say unto you, that every idle word that men shall speak, they shall give account thereof in the day of judgment. For by thy words thou shalt be justified, and by thy words, thou shalt be condemned."–Matthew 12:36-37.

When you request something, you better be specific, because what you say is what you'll get. In our prayer life, we mess this up a lot. We pray about the problem, not the solution, so we get more of what we don't want... problems.

Confess excellent health, strength, happiness, favor, confidence, talent, success, prosperity, integrity, blessings, victory, etc. You know what you want in life, call those things that not be as though they were.

Proverbs 12:21

"There shall no evil happen to the just: but the wicked shall be filled with mischief."

As a believer and walking with God, not every day will be wine and roses. Uncomfortable situations arise, and unfortunate things happen. However, if we keep our faith and continue to believe then we have the confidence, we will come out on top. No matter what it looks like, no matter how hard it gets, no matter the opposition, if God is FOR us, then He is more than the entire world AGAINST us.

Trials, tribulations, and evil will sometimes come but if we keep our faith in God and trust him, we will be able to stand. "Finally, my brethren, be strong in the Lord, and in the power of his might. Put on the whole armour of God, that ye may be able to stand against the wiles of the devil. For we wrestle not against flesh and blood, but against principalities, against powers, against the rulers of the darkness of this world, against spiritual wickedness in high places."–Ephesians 6:10-12.

Wicked people appear to flourish by doing their sinful deeds however, their time will come when they must give an account for all their foolish ways and God will place judgment. God places a covering on the righteous. What does that mean for you? It means that the Father looks out for His children.

Chapter Thirteen

Proverbs 13:7

"There is that maketh himself rich, yet hath nothing: there is that maketh himself poor, yet hath great riches."

Are you witnessing your true financial status on the outside or are you a fraud?

I remember listening to a sermon by T. D. Jakes once where he spoke about people pretending to be something they aren't. People who were driving expensive fancy cars with elaborate rims but were living in an apartment. People like this are pretending to be something they are not. What's wrong with driving a Prius instead of a BMW? Granted "Jeff" Dunham the talented American ventriloquist and comedian likes to have one of his puppets Peanut make fun of the Prius car, but the bottom line is it will take you where you need to go just like any other car. Why don't you take that money you are paying for those expensive cars every month as a car payment and invest in a down payment on a home? At least if the economy ever went belly up you can take a loan on your home to keep you afloat until the economy rebounds.

Why do you care what people think about what you drive, how you dress, what type of jewelry you wear, etc.? When you worry about these things and stress about what people think about you, then you are not using wisdom.

On the other side of the coin, there are wealthy people who pretend they are poor so they can hoard everything. These people choose not to be a blessing. They would rather make people believe they are poor and down on their luck instead of acknowledging that they are affluent and being grateful to God for what he has blessed them with. When you are blessed with wealth, then it is your responsibility to be a blessing to others. There is no more clear-cut example of a person who realizes this than Oprah Winfrey.

Proverbs 13:13

"Whoso despiseth the word shall be destroyed: but he that feareth the commandment shall be rewarded."

There was a man named Smith Wigglesworth who was a British Evangelist who had this to say about the Bible. "The Bible is the Word of God: Supernatural in origin, eternal in duration, inexpressible in valor, infinite in scope, regenerative in power, infallible in authority, universal in interest, personal in application, and inspired in totality. Read it through, write it down, pray it in, work it out, and then pass it on."

It is vital we have the Lord's counsel in all aspects of our lives. If we go it alone, we will encounter tragic results. The Holy Spirit lives within us and is our internal GPS system and is there to assist and guide us. Use what the Lord has given you to bless you.

Proverbs 13:22

"A good man leaveth an inheritance to his children's children: and the wealth of the sinner is laid up for the just."

Solomon is telling us here that as parents we are responsible to not only leave an inheritance to our children but to our grandchildren. Now, this is not just monetary. Let's look at the monetary side first. David originated as a shepherd boy and ended as a Godly king. David made a point to transfer the throne, along with the kingdom and all his wealth to his children. Parents should desire to make sure that their kids are better off than they were. Unfortunately, in today's world, there are many people who pass away without having a will and this leaves a tremendous burden on their children. They have enough to deal with especially if the death was sudden.

We also must prepare our children spiritually as King David did for Solomon. Our heavenly father expects the next generation to advance not to decline. Just look at the example of Jesus and how he tapped into everything his father God taught him.

Proverbs 13:24

"He that spareth his rod hateth his son: but he that loveth him chasteneth him betimes."

Are you afraid to discipline your children? If so, then you are not showing your children you care about them and how they turn out in life. Discipline does not mean spankings but when needed that should be done. This new thing about timeout is not the answer! When we are unwilling to correct our children, it appears we don't love them and when you love your children disciplining them is necessary. As parents that are believers in God, we must take the time and make a conscious effort to show our children we love them by correcting their mistakes when they are erroneous. You don't want to wait until your children are adults to discipline them because by then they may not hear what you have to say. Or by that time they will wind up on TV shows like Jerry Springer. Now let me stress this point Jerry always has words of wisdom for his guests at the end of his show but these are things they should have been taught by their parent's ages ago and now it's too late. It's like the old saying you don't wait until the horse gets out of the barn to lock up the gate.

I remember when I was five years old; I went to the supermarket with my grandmother. Now, this was not the first time I had gone with her and the supermarket was about 5-6 blocks from where we lived. While in the supermarket with her she angered me and so I walked away and left her there and walked home. I thought I was grown. My father however later in the day showed me how grown I was and gave me a beating. This was significant in my life because I had never had a beating from my father before that day and never had one again from him. I learned from that beating I must respect my elders and that I was just a child but more importantly my grandmother was terrified that something bad had happened to me or I was abducted. In the world in which we live today, there are so many amber alerts and child abductions that this lesson many years ago taught me a lot.

"And ye have forgotten the exhortation which speaketh unto you as unto children, my son, despise not thou the chastening of the Lord, nor faint when thou art rebuked of him: For whom the Lord loveth he chasteneth, and scourgeth every son whom he receiveth. If ye endure chastening, God dealeth with you as with sons; for what son is he whom the father chasteneth not?"–Hebrews 12:5-7.

Book of Proverbs

Chapter Fourteen

Proverbs 14:7

"Go from the presence of a foolish man, when thou perceivest not in him the lips of knowledge."

Keep your distance from fools. You will know them by their words. Foolish people prefer to hear themselves talk. The Lord inspired Solomon to write Proverbs to teach you wisdom for successful living. When a person speaks, and their words are the opposite of God's words that is a red alert. A tremendous amount of young people has been corrupted by bad friends and peer pressure. Parents instruct your children, so they are not sucked into things that their friends say and do.

"The fool hath said in his heart, there is no God. They are corrupt; they have done abominable works, there is none that doeth good."–Psalm 14:1. "Be not hasty in thy spirit to be angry: for anger resteth in the bosom of fools."–Ecclesiastes 7:9. "And everyone that heareth these sayings of mine, and doeth them not, shall be likened unto a foolish man, which built his house upon the sand: And the rain descended, and the floods came, and the winds blew, and beat upon that house; and it fell: and great was the fall of it."–Matthew 7: 26-27.

Any sane person realizes that you don't build your home on the sand especially in today's climate. The destruction of homes that were built with a firm foundation in the last few years that have been destroyed due to hurricanes has been horrific. If anyone were to do this thing, they would be a prime example of a fool. Follow God, study the word, and stay clear from people that speak foolishly.

Proverbs 14:17

"He that is soon angry dealeth foolishly: and a man of wicked devices is hated."

There are two kinds of anger. Rash anger, by a quick temper that reacts without discretion or thought. People that are quick-tempered have no self-control. Then there is another kind of anger, malice. These are the people that hold revenge deep in their heart and plot to harm others.

Back in the day, we used to see a lot of the first type of anger more often. Couples who got into fights and arguments and then physical abuse started and the police had to be called to the home. This still happens but the second type of anger has gained much more notoriety lately. A prime example of this is the 2017 Las Vegas Shootings. God despises this type of anger. This type of sin is long-term conceiving wickedness.

How do you stay away from falling into this trap of anger? You must learn how to rule your spirit. Now, this is one of those things you must work on, grow into, and pray to God daily to help you with your temper. Being a Type A Personality myself this is something I have had to work on. My husband will tell you I have improved but there is still work to be done

Most women can appreciate what I am about to say. They ask their husband to do something and they take forever to complete it. Here is a personal account of my own. I was born and raised in New York. I met my husband there as well. In 2002 we moved from New York to Florida. Now I'm sure that most places if not all cities and states have roaches, mice, and rats. I was familiar with these, however, moving to Florida I became familiar with lizards. Now I took a while to get used to them, but I did. As long as they stayed on their turf and not invading mine, we were all good. However, they believed they could hang out in my mailbox. Every time I would go to get the mail and I opened the box they would jump out at me and scare me. I advised my husband promptly of this and told him he needed to cement the mailbox, so they could not keep getting in there. If they were not paying the bills for the household, they did not belong in my mailbox! From the first time, I asked my husband to take care of the mailbox until he finally executed the job was four years. I don't have to tell you how many times my anger went ballistic on him even though he was now getting the mail from the mailbox because I refused to do it. But you know there were many days he forgot. I went to bed early one night which is normally not me because I am a night person, but I woke up because I was thirsty, and my husband was nowhere to be found. After about 15 minutes he came through the front door. It was 1am. I asked him where he was, and he told me he was outside cementing the mailbox. I looked at him and shook my head and thought to myself yes, your mother named you with the correct letter P for Patrick and Procrastinator and went back to bed.

Proverbs 14:25

"A true witness delivereth souls: but a deceitful witness speaketh lies."

Every day courts are full of trials taking place to determine if a person is guilty or innocent. Every day we all can tell the truth or tell a lie. God is expecting all of us to be truthful and honorable people. He gave us the greatest example Jesus.

Most of us have heard the story of Pinocchio. Pinocchio had a very short nose but every time he was under stress or decided to lie his nose would grow. Wouldn't this be the perfect weapon in courtrooms today to determine if a witness or defendant were telling the truth or lying? If only life could be so simple.

The greatest trial of all time is approaching. All men shall give an account of their lives to God. It is very important to set your heart and mouth to always tell the truth.

Proverbs 14:26

"In the fear of the Lord is strong confidence: and his children shall have a place of refuge."

"The angel of the Lord encampeth round about them that fear him, and delivereth them."–Psalm 34:7. People who fear the Lord are the safest men and women on earth. They obey and worship the Lord God, and they know He is always with them.

David had the courage and was fearless when he had to face Goliath. Daniel had no fear when he was thrown into the lion's den. Shadrach, Meshach, and Abednego did not fear King Nebuchadnezzar and refused to bow down to him and were thrown into the fiery furnace and survived. If you have never heard of this story in the bible, read it. You can find it in the book of Daniel 3:10-28.

People who fear the Lord are the most healthy and sound people on earth. These people conform and honor God and are confident that the Lord walks with them.

These are stories of great confidence and bravery, but Jesus Christ was the boldest of them all. He went to the cross for all of us.

Proverbs 14:29

"He that is slow to wrath is of great understanding: but he that is hasty of spirit exalteth folly."

Are you the type of person that is quick to get angry where your blood bubbles and boils up inside you? Is your anger sometimes so fierce that you want to lash out at everybody and anybody? If so, then you are placing yourself in the classification of a fool. Wisdom requires you to have self-control over your spirit. Anger or wrath is an intense negative emotion. Anger places people in jail, anger sometimes places people in hospitals to be treated for cuts, wounds, gunshots, etc.

Anger is not always wrong; however, you need to know how to control yourself. I'm sure a lot of you have heard the saying "don't go to bed angry." This is a powerful statement. Life is short, and you never know when you will draw your last breath. This is one I have been working on for years. You married women will know what I mean. When your spouse doesn't do what you ask them to do time after time and you blow up on them slam the bedroom door and refuse to speak. Well, tomorrow will come but it doesn't mean your spouse will be there to say I'm sorry or we need to discuss what happened in a calm matter. I know many of you know people who have had tremendous fights and said a lot of things they didn't mean and later wanted to take them back and never had the chance to.

So, what am I saying you should replace your anger with? Do whatever brings you happiness and joy that is not against God's laws. If you like to play basketball, go do that if you like to read pick up a good book, if you are like me and enjoy movies then go to the movies. Do whatever takes away the anger and cool off until you can be rational and handle things peacefully and tranquil. Don't be foolish it could wind up being very costly and detrimental.

Chapter Fifteen

Proverbs 15:3

"The eyes of the Lord are in every place, beholding the evil and the good."

You have decided to quit smoking but whenever nobody is around; you keep sneaking in a cigarette. You have decided to quit drinking, but you keep a flask hidden that nobody knows about. You are trying to make your marriage work and swore to your spouse I will not have another affair, but you are getting out of bed and picking up your clothes from off the hotel floor where you were with a person who was not your spouse. You pledged you would never gamble again but here you are in the casino throwing the dice. Well, nobody you know has seen you do these things, but God was watching every move.

"Know ye not that ye are the temple of God, and that the Spirit of God dwelleth in you?"–1 Corinthians 3:16. "But if the Spirit of him that raised up Jesus from the dead dwell in you, he that raised up Christ from the dead shall also quicken your mortal bodies by his Spirit that dwelleth in you."–Romans 8:11. "That good thing which was committed unto thee keep by the Holy Ghost which dwelleth in us."–2 Timothy 1:14. "For the eyes of the Lord run to and fro throughout the whole earth, to shew himself strong in the behalf of them whose heart is perfect toward him. Herein thou hast done foolishly: therefore, from henceforth thou shalt have wars." 2 Chronicles 16:9.

In this era of modern technology with camera drones, smart tv's, Alexa, etc. with all the info and things they can see how can you not see that God sees all things. There was a report back on May 25, 2018, by reporter Gary Horcher that stated a woman in Portland, Ore., told KIRO7, a television news station in Washington, that her Amazon Echo device had recorded a conversation then shared it with one of her husband's employees in Seattle. Now, Amazon says it knows what happened: As the woman, identified only as Danielle, chatted away with her husband, the device's virtual assistant, Alexa, mistakenly heard a series of requests and commands to send the recording as a voice message to one of the husband's employees.

God created this world and everything in it, so he knows all things we all do, what we all say, how we treat people when we try to hide. He lives inside us all so every time we are hiding; he is right there hiding along with us. Every lie we tell he is there to hear the lie. The same way a cell phone can track where you are God's tracking device is the best.

Proverbs 15:4

"A wholesome tongue is a tree of life: but perverseness therein is a breach in the spirit."

Are people delighted to be around you and hear what you have to say, or do they shy away from you? Do people normally request your advice on things? Do people feel uplifted and happy when they speak to you or are, they disappointed and feeling like they came out of a sword fight?

You either restore and encourage with your words, or you inflict pain and damage. You either teach and train and elevate, or you degrade and cause discomfort.

I live in Florida and they have a theme park down here called Legoland. Now Legos are building blocks that the Lego company states "inspires and develops the builders of tomorrow." This is what God wants us to do for others. We are to inspire them and build them up with our words not degrade and diminish them.

This proverb has another lesson: your mouth can only say what is in your heart. How you feel deep within is what you display on the outside. God endowed you with a tongue to extol him and assist others. How will you address and speak to people in life today? You should not speak unless you have something beneficial and positive to say. Your reputation depends on what you say today.

Proverbs 15:15

"All the days of the afflicted are evil: but he that is of a merry heart hath a continual feast."

We must be content with what we presently have because when God sees that then he knows he can bless us with more. I'm sure we all know people that no matter what they have they still find something to complain about. This recalls the following quotes.

"I cried because I had no shoes until I met a man who had no feet."–Helen Keller.

"I live in the space of thankfulness — and I have been rewarded a million times over. I started out giving thanks for small things, and the more thankful I became, the more my bounty increased. That's because for sure what you focus on expands. When you focus on the goodness in life, you create more of it." –Oprah Winfrey

We all need to look at the glass half full instead of half empty. We all have so much to be grateful for.

A few years ago, I had the privilege of being in the presence of a man named Nick Vujicic he was a special guest speaker at the church I attend in Orlando FL. If you are unaware of this man, he was born with tetra-amelia syndrome which is a rare disorder (called phocomelia) characterized by the absence of arms and legs. Vujicic has two small and deformed feet, one of which he calls his "chicken drumstick" because of its shape. He is a 39-year-old evangelist and motivational speaker who has been married since 2012 and has 4 children.

How you should live your life is having a merry heart and a continual feast and being grateful for what you have because that is what will propel God to give you more.

Proverbs 15:22

"Without counsel purposes are disappointed: but in the multitude of counsellors they are established."

If your doctor advised you that you need spine surgery would you do it without asking a second, third, maybe even a fourth opinion? If you won, the lottery for millions of dollars would you get advice from one financial planner on what to do with your money and who to invest it with?

The above are major decisions you wouldn't make lightheartedly. You would ask multiple people for their advice before you made a final decision. People make plans to get married, start a business, go back to school, buy a house, find a church, homeschool children, make a career change, borrow money and much more. When you orchestrate your future, you are partial towards the conclusion. It is vital you envelope yourself with well-informed, prudent, calm, decisive people to make recommendations for you.

One of the greatest movies ever made that was released in 2017 was titled "The Greatest Showman." The film is inspired by the story of P. T. Barnum's creation of the Barnum & Bailey Circus (1871–2017) and the lives of its star attractions. It took seven years to complete this movie and there were meetings on top of meetings involving everyone who had anything to do with the creation of this movie. What was the outcome? A production that had a budget of $84 million dollars but had a box office of $434.6 million. They would never have had that tremendous success if there wasn't extensive research, multiple meetings, patience, and getting input from every resource available to them.

Book of Proverbs

Chapter Sixteen

Proverbs 16:3

"Commit thy works unto the Lord, and thy thoughts shall be established."

The way in which you commit your works unto the Lord is by entrusting all your ideas, plans, ventures to him. You place all of them in God's loving hands knowing and having faith he will do what is in your best interest always.

Now for many of us, this can be a very daunting task because we always want to be in charge and control of everything. When you live a life for Christ you are never in control. All of us have encountered a time in our lives where we were very stressed and no matter what we tried it didn't work out as we wanted it to. The results depend on God. Jesus gave us a prime example of this when he was on a ship with the disciples sleeping. "And there arose a great storm of wind, and the waves beat into the ship, so it was now full. And he was in the hinder part of the ship, asleep on a pillow: and they awake him, and say unto him, Master, carest thou not that we perish? And he arose, and rebuked the wind, and said unto the sea, Peace, be still. And the wind ceased, and there was a great calm. And he said unto them, why are ye so fearful? how is it that ye have no faith? And they feared exceedingly, and said one to another, What manner of man is this, that even the wind and the sea obey him?"–Mark 4:37-41.

God cares about our heart's desire from the smallest thing to the biggest thing and he can handle every situation and provide for our every need. Two years ago, I wanted to replace the coffee table in our living room, but I wanted a table that was a lift top so when my husband was writing his invoices for work, he didn't have to bend his back. I walked into Kane's furniture store with my husband and looked around. We were only in the store for minutes when I came upon the exact table I wanted. My husband sat on the sofa in front of the table and the height was perfect with the lift top of the table. It was also on sale, so it was a win-win.

Trust God for everything and commit your works unto him from the smallest to the largest and he will take care of you.

Proverbs 16:7

"When a man's ways please the Lord, he maketh even his enemies to be at peace with him."

If you do your best to live a moral life God will make even your enemies, be at peace with you. We all have enemies. It could be a family member, a co-worker, or a neighbor, etc. Even in biblical times, characters in the Bible had enemies. God changed Laban's thoughts, and he became peaceable with his son-in-law Jacob. God melted Esau's heart to be loving towards his brother Jacob. Joseph was able to remain peaceful with his master Potiphar.

We celebrated a monumental Olympics in 2018. The Olympics brought North and South Korea together. Athletes from the two Koreas marched into the stadium together offering hope of a breakthrough in a tense, geopolitical standoff that has stirred fears of nuclear conflict. Many considered it an impossible dream to have an Olympics of peace, in which North Korea would take part and the two Koreas would form a joint team, but it happened. The LORD Himself will calm agitated enemies and protect you from violent ones for your obedience. Trust in God.

Proverbs 16:17

"The highway of the upright is to depart from evil: he that keepeth his way preserveth his soul."

Every day we make many choices. We can either do what is right and live a godly life which is what God wants from us all or we can follow wicked devices and take the highway to hell. If you find yourself on the wrong highway depart quickly because it will only bring you grief. The more you remain on the highway of the upright the more it will bless you.

When you leave the supermarket put the shopping cart in the designated spot instead of leaving it anywhere it can roll and hit someone's car. Saying the magic words thank you when you receive service from someone. You witness that someone has left their cell phone on the table in the restaurant you both were eating in. Don't ignore it and say it's not mine get up and return it to them. You Park in a parking lot where you are about to go see a concert and you are running late but the car next to you who also just parked left their headlights on. Call out to them and advise them instead of saying I'm already late. These are examples of simple things you do when you are on the highway of the upright.

Daily it tempts us to make wrong choices, but we must do like Jesus did when he was being tempted by Satan in the wilderness for 40 days and 40 nights. We must stand strong and finish strong. God gives us all a fresh set of grace every 24 hours to propel us to make it through.

Proverbs 16:20

"He that handleth a matter wisely shall find good: and whoso trusteth in the Lord, happy is he."

Wisdom and faith are what will bring you success in life.

They define wisdom as good sense; a wise attitude, belief, or course of action, the ability to discern inner qualities and relationships.

They define faith as a firm belief in something for which there is no proof, complete trust, belief, and trust in and loyalty to God.

How do you get wisdom? You ask God for it the same way Solomon did. "In that night did God appear unto Solomon, and said unto him, ask what I shall give thee. And Solomon said unto God, thou hast shewed great mercy unto David my father, and hast made me to reign in his stead. Now, O Lord God, let thy promise unto David my father be established: for thou hast made me king over a people like the dust of the earth in multitude. Give me now wisdom and knowledge, that I may go out and come in before this people: for who can judge this thy people, that is so great? And God said to Solomon, Because this was in thine heart, and thou hast not asked riches, wealth, or honour, nor the life of thine enemies, neither yet hast asked long life; but hast asked wisdom and knowledge for thyself, that thou mayest judge my people, over whom I have made thee king: Wisdom and knowledge is granted unto thee; and I will give thee riches, and wealth, and honour, such as none of the kings have had that have been before thee, neither shall there any after thee have the like."– 2 Chronicles 1:7-12.

How do you get faith? You ask God for it and believe you will receive it. "And all things, whatsoever ye shall ask in prayer, believing, ye shall receive."–Matthew 21:22. "Now faith is the substance of things hoped for, the evidence of things not seen."– Hebrews 11:1. "That your faith should not stand in the wisdom of men, but in the power of God."–1 Corinthians 2:5.

Pick up your Bible and read it. Don't just let it sit out for show when you have company, or the elders of your church stop by. Read Hebrews Chapter 11 in its entirety. That talks about the faith of so many people in the Bible. It will encourage and strengthen you as you go through your daily life.

I live in one of the top ten travel destination states in the United States. The Sunshine State of Florida. There is a host of various attributes it has such as great beaches, world-class hotels, world-renowned restaurants, Disney World, Kennedy Space Center, spring training baseball and regular season baseball which is one of my passions but that's a subject for another time. There is also Universal Studios in Orlando FL which houses the Hollywood Rip Ride Rockit, The Incredible Hulk, and the Kid-sized Woody

Woodpecker roller coasters. Roller Coasters has become one of the mandatory rides for the thrill-seekers whenever they visit amusement parks. They have become an engineering marvel, and have been constructed to be taller, faster, and wilder than ever. They say one of the languages of love is French so for thrill-seekers they call it "amateurs de sensations fortes". Why is it though we climb into the roller coaster giddy, sweaty, pumped with adrenaline and faith that the ride will be awesome! We never have wavering faith that our feet will never land safely on solid ground within 3 1/2 to 4 minutes after the ride's inception. So, if we are so confident and stable and grounded in our faith in a man-made steel object why is our faith so flimsy in our creator? So, I have a question for you to ponder, if GOD created man and endowed him with powerful knowledge to create roller coasters shouldn't we have the strongest unfailing faith in GOD?

Chapter Seventeen

Proverbs 17:5

"Whoso mocketh the poor reproacheth his Maker: and he that is glad at calamities shall not be unpunished."

There is an old saying do unto others as you would have them do unto you. In the bible, they list this verse as "Therefore all things whatsoever ye would that men should do to you, do ye even so to them: for this is the law and the prophets."–Matthew 7-12.

If you are blessed with use of all your five senses, if you have all your limbs for use, if you have a home or apartment to go to and somewhere to lay your head you are blessed. If you can get your own meals and don't have to depend on a service like Meals on Wheels, if you have a washer and dryer where you live, and you don't have to go to a laundromat, if you have a car, motorcycle, bicycle, or other means of transportation where you don't have to wait on a bus or train you are blessed. If you are gifted to have athleticism, if you have a staggering financial net worth where you can be a blessing to others, if both of your elderly parents are still alive and not living in a nursing home or in an assisted living place you are blessed.

As you can see, there are so many ways in which God blesses us and we should never mock or make fun of someone who has less than what we have. We are to be grateful and thankful because it can be taken away at any moment. That is something we have all either encountered or have seen or heard about on TV. A good example of this is hurricanes. In recent years we had major hurricanes like Harvey, Irma, Maria and Ida that did tremendous damage and cost a major loss of life. Many people lost most if not all their possessions starting with their homes. For those who were fortunate to not lose their homes, they were blessed.

God frowns on individuals that tease or mock regarding acts of God surrounding others. God's grace he has placed on your life is because of his favor. "Every good gift and every perfect gift is from above, and cometh down from the Father of lights, with whom is no variableness, neither shadow of turning."–James 1:17.

Proverbs 17:9

"He that covereth a transgression seeketh love; but he that repeateth a matter separateth very friends."

When you love someone, it is vital you learn how to forgive and forget. This is when you overlook things that people have done to you personally. We all have slip ups where we have let anger get the best of us and hurt someone. It never feels good to have a constant reminder from those we have hurt regarding what we did. So, we should not continue to hold it over people's head when they have hurt us. This is an area of my life I have been working on for years and I still have a way to go but recently I encountered an excellent example I believe will help me progress faster where forgiveness is concerned.

I went to the movies awhile back and saw the film Unbroken: Path to Redemption. Haunted by nightmares of his torment, Louie sees himself as anything but a hero. Then, he meets Cynthia, a young woman who captures his eye and his heart. Louie's quest for revenge drives him deeper into despair, putting the couple on the brink of divorce until Cynthia experiences Billy Graham's 1949 Los Angeles Crusade, where both find faith in Jesus Christ, a renewed commitment to their marriage, and Louie finds forgiveness for his wartime captors. This is a powerful movie with an even more powerful message about forgiveness that everyone should see.

Proverbs 17:20

"He that hath a froward heart findeth no good: and he that hath a perverse tongue falleth into mischief."

An unfavorable heart or evil speech brings distress. We must remember that death and life are in the power of the tongue so we must watch the things that come out of our mouth because it can lead you to destruction and mischief. The Bible tells us that whatever is in our heart is what will spill out of our mouth. "O generation of vipers, how can ye, being evil, speak good things? for out of the abundance of the heart the mouth speaketh."– Matthew 12:34.

God does not approve of this way of life. In the book of Numbers in the Bible, there is a great example of how God will not stand for this. Aaron and Miriam found fault with Moses for his Ethiopian wife, so God made Miriam white with leprosy.

We are all aware of the serial killer Jeffrey Dahmer who was known as the Milwaukee Cannibal or the Milwaukee Monster, was an American serial killer and sex offender, who committed the rape, murder, and dismemberment of 17 men and boys from 1978 to 1991. Many of his later murders involved necrophilia, cannibalism, and the permanent preservation of body parts typically all or part of the skeleton. –Wikipedia (Jeffrey Dahmer). This is a man who had an unfavorable heart.

If you wish to experience well in life, you must learn to guard your heart and your tongue.

Proverbs 17:25

"A foolish son is a grief to his father, and bitterness to her that bare him."

Parents may find great suffering in the absurd and trifling character of their children. Due to the maternal instinct and bond, there is a special pain and galling that belongs to the mother of a ridiculous son or daughter. Mothers suffer much pain giving birth to a child and it makes them distraught when that child turns out to be an ungodly child. One of the Ten Commandments states "Honor Thy Father and Thy Mother." You are to respect your parents and treat them with honor and dignity.

Why did you have children? Is it so you can collect thousands of dollars at tax season? If that is the case, then you never should have had them! I remember my mother said God rest her soul after she gave birth and returned home from the hospital with me, she lifted me up to the heavens and said, "God I give her back to you to mold and do with her as you please."

A lot of the problem with today's children is that their parents are children themselves. You have children raising children. I was speaking with a young woman recently who is living proof of this situation. She is unmarried and became pregnant when she was 21 years old. She gave birth to her daughter at 22. She said when she advised her mother; she was pregnant her mother didn't speak to her for 3 months she was so upset. This young woman is now 29 years old, her daughter is 7 years old, and her mother is 51 years old about to be 52 years old. When this young woman's daughter was born her mother became a 45-year-old grandmother. Things have evolved and the three of them are very happy together and this young woman stated even though her mother was so angry with her she was still the first person to purchase baby gifts for her granddaughter.

Parents be a constant intercessor for your children. Children due your due diligence and give the utmost respect and honor to your parents. This is the Godly way.

Proverbs 17:28

"Even a fool, when he holdeth his peace, is counted wise: and he that shutteth his lips is esteemed a man of understanding."

Overly eager speech, unplanned speech, or too much speech can make you appear to be a person lacking in judgment or prudence.

Keeping quiet and speaking less will cause others to assume you are a person of wisdom and great understanding.

This is exactly the reason God gave us all two ears and one mouth. We are to listen more and talk less. The tongue is dangerous and easily hurts others. It is better to be quick to respond via hearing than at speaking. Wise people learn how to rule over their tongue and be judicious.

Composed in Sanskrit in India around 300 CE, the Panchatantram is one of the oldest collections of fables in the world. There is a story called "The Turtle Who Couldn't Stop Talking" that I will recount here. Long, long ago, a turtle lived in a pond with two swans. The turtle loved to talk. She always had something to say, and she liked to hear herself say it.

After they had lived in the pond happily for many years, a dry spell came. There was no rain for weeks and weeks. At last the pond dried up completely. The two swans realized they would have to leave their home and fly to another pond with water. They went to say good-bye to their friend, the turtle. But she begged them, "Don't leave me behind! I too have nothing to eat and no water to live on. I will surely die if I am left here."

"But you can't fly!" said the swans. "How can we take you with us?"

"Take me with you! Please take me with you!" pleaded the turtle.

The swans felt so sorry for their friend that at last they came up with a plan. They said to the turtle, "We have thought of a way to take you with us. We will each take hold of one end of a long stick. You must hold onto the middle of it with your beak and never let go. You must not talk as long as we are carrying you! If you open your mouth, you'll fall to the ground."

The turtle promised not to say a word. Away the swans flew into the air carrying the turtle on the stick between them. As they rose above the treetops, the turtle wanted to say, "Goodness, look how high we are!" but she remembered the swans' warning.

Soon they passed over a small town, and a few people looked up and shouted, "Look at the swans carrying a turtle! What a silly sight!"

The turtle thought to herself, "Why don't they mind their own business?" but she remembered not to say anything out loud.

Soon more villagers came to see the sight. They cried, "How strange! A flying turtle! Look, everybody!"

The turtle could stand it no longer. She opened her mouth to call out, "Hush, you foolish people!" But as she did, she let go of the stick and fell to the ground. She landed on her back, and her shell cracked into a thousand pieces.

Turtle's shell has remained that way to this day. Her cracked shell reminds us of what can happen if we talk too much.

I'm sure you get the gist of what I am saying.

Book of Proverbs

Chapter Eighteen

Proverbs 18:4

"The words of a man's mouth are as deep waters and the wellspring of wisdom as a flowing brook."

Do you consider yourself a deep and flowing person? A wise person has depth of wisdom and knows how to provide wise advice. The first part of this proverb declares that a wise man's words are like deep waters. A wise person's words are not shallow but are deep and penetrating to the soul. A person of wisdom can assist with different predicaments. The second part of this proverb states that a wise person's words are like a wellspring just as a flowing brook. A wellspring is a source of continual supply. When something is flowing, it is moving smoothly and continuously. A brook is a small stream. This is what a person of wisdom offers with their words.

Now Solomon was precisely this person. People came from all over to listen to his wisdom. Now you need not be a walking dictionary or encyclopedia or even a facsimile of a Jeopardy contestant. You need to be knowledgeable enough to recognize that every good gift comes from God and wisdom is the greatest of them all. Get into the habit of saying, God, when I open my mouth please speak for me and he will.

Proverbs 18:20

"A man's belly shall be satisfied with the fruit of his mouth; and with the increase of his lips shall he be filled."

Do you dream? Of course, you do. The definition of a dream is something notable for its beauty, excellence, or enjoyable quality. It also signifies a strongly desired goal or purpose. Do you crave to be fortunate and prosperous? It is possible! All you need to do is learn how to talk better. Concentrate on improving the words you use and the more conscientious you are about it God will bless you.

Train yourself to speak and talk about what you want not what you have. If you are single and want to be married talk about the great life you have coming soon with your future spouse. Don't keep speaking about how lonely you are and must come home to an empty place every night with no one to cuddle with or talk with. This will only continue to bring you more of what you have right now. Don't keep complaining about your old beat-up car. Be grateful you have one! Care for it and maintain it but dream and put a vision in your head of the new car you want and how it will feel once you have it. Think about the new car smell and the heated seats. Don't keep complaining about how old the car is and how you must leave the house so much earlier in the morning to get the car started to go to work. Think about all the people who must take the bus or train or walk even. The more you talk about or meditate on the things you don't want the more of them you will get. If you are having issues with your health instead of complaining about it every day say thank you for my healing.

I could go on and on about this one proverb because this will truly be the breakthrough in your life once you master it. Like anything else, this also requires forming a habit. They say if you do something for a 30-day period then it will become second nature. Once you start, you may be good for two days before something throws you off course. It can be something as simple as saying everybody in my office has a cold, so I know I will get it soon. The minute you realize what you said reverse it and say instead I am grateful God has his arms of protection around me, so I will not get sick.

Now know Satan will attack you daily on this one. Why? It is the basis of God creating the world. The words of his mouth brought everything into existence. Now once you have success with this hold, those successes close to your heart and remember them. You may even get a journal and write them down. It can be as simple as you saying I declare in the name of Jesus that I will not run into traffic going to work today. I declare in the name of Jesus that when I go grocery shopping after work, I will not wind up in the line with people that have lots of coupons and I must be there forever. I declare in the name of Jesus that when I go to the ATM at the bank, there will be enough money for it to process my withdrawal transaction.

As you have small successes, you will want to up the ante and get bolder. However, that is not something you have to wait to do. Remember, in Matthew 7:7 it says, "ask and it shall be given you." Now, do I believe this, and has it worked for me? Absolutely it has. I was 14 years old and lying in bed listening to a New York radio station WBLS with a disc jockey named Vaughn Harper at night with a program the radio station called "The Quiet Storm" which featured love songs and I remember saying I want to marry a man tall, dark, and handsome who speaks French. This is how quick your prayers and words can be answered. I married my husband 7 years later when I was 21 years old. We have been married now for 37 years. Oh, and yes my husband Patrick is 6'2, dark-skinned, handsome, and is from Haiti where they speak Creole and French.

Proverbs 18:21

"Death and life are in the power of the tongue: and they that love it shall eat the fruit thereof."

Your words will either assist or destroy you. If you have passed your adolescence years, then it already has. When you speak your words will either bring encouragement or demolishment. Your tongue can ruin or preserve people's lives.

Throughout your life, you will encounter people who are struggling tremendously because they did not know how to control their tongue. These people caused their fruit to die. Instead of using their tongue to uplift them and bless their lives they used their tongue to destroy them.

Then there are those that seem to flourish because they knew how to control their speech. They realized that if what they were about to say was not a positive affirmation, then just choke it off and don't speak.

Are you a person who people yearn to be around and want to speak with? If people constantly want to run the other way and hide from you that should tell you something. Wives if your husbands can't wait for a lady's night out where they don't have to see you or speak to you for a while that is a sign. Children if your teachers in school get excited when you do something that requires detention or suspension, so they can get a break from you then you are not a desirable person to be around.

The good news is you can change, and God can help you. You can change your life. You can change how people see you. People can see you in a better light. Proverbs 18:20 & 21 are similar, and I felt the need to address them both because they can shape your life.

Proverbs 18:22

"Whoso findeth a wife findeth a good thing, and obtaineth favour of the Lord."

"And the Lord God said, it is not good that the man should be alone; I will make him an help meet for him."–Genesis 2:18. "And the Lord God caused a deep sleep to fall upon Adam, and he slept: and he took one of his ribs and closed up the flesh instead thereof; And the rib, which the Lord God had taken from man, made he a woman, and brought her unto the man. And Adam said, this is now bone of my bones, and flesh of my flesh: she shall be called Woman, because she was taken out of Man. Therefore, shall a man leave his father and his mother, and shall cleave unto his wife: and they shall be one flesh."–Genesis 2:21-24.

Even though God created the perfect world where there was no sickness, pain, sin, or trouble; with healthy nutrition, he desired for Adam to have a mate. Adam needed a perfect companion to help him maximize his life in this world.

If you are a married man and are fortunate to have a wife that truly loves God and has committed her life to him be grateful. Women, it should be as clear as a rainbow in the sky if you are doing right by your husband. If you are you will see it by your husband's happiness and your reputation with others.

Chapter Nineteen

Proverbs 19:1

"Better is the poor that walketh in his integrity, than he that is perverse in his lips, and is a fool."

Integrity - firm adherence to a code of especially moral or artistic values; an unimpaired condition.

Are you a person of integrity? Do you have a strict code of morality? Every day daily we are presented with integrity choices. Are you willing to lie on a job application so you can get the job? Even though you raise your hand in court and swore to tell the whole truth and nothing but the truth, do you? You are desperate for a loan? Are you willing to lie to the bank or financial institution instead of trusting God for a beneficial outcome? Your goal in life should be to always reflect integrity. This is something that should be reflected in every aspect of your life.

Nabal was a man in the bible who was remarkable in magnitude and very wealthy. He also had a beautiful wife named Abigail. There is a story about him and David and how David needed his assistance for provision. The story goes on to say that David sent men to Nabal requesting food and supplies while he and his men were on the run from King Saul. Nabal sent a message of decline and insults back with David's men to inform David. David told all his men to prepare to attach Nabal but one of David's men advised Nabal's wife Abigail what was about to happen. Abigail moved speedily and put together all the provisions David requested and loaded them on donkeys and advised her servants to go to David and she followed them. David was pleased and thanked her and advised his men to return to their camp. Nabal and his family and others were saved because of Abigail's actions although Nabal did not know what his wife had done. Nabal got intoxicated that night and was still unaware of what happened. The next day when he was sober again Abigail advised him what she had done, and his heart immediately weakened and ten days later God struck Nabal and he died.

Living a life of integrity is always the most prudent thing to do.

Proverbs 19:17

"He that hath pity upon the poor lendeth unto the Lord; and that which he hath given will he pay him again."

Financial success is easy. When you give to the poor God will bless you. Assisting those that are financially challenged is the godly thing to do. If you give money freely and happily God will bless you. "There is that scattereth, and yet increaseth; and there is that withholdeth more than is meet, but it tendeth to poverty. The liberal soul shall be made fat: and he that watereth shall be watered also himself. He that withholdeth corn, the people shall curse him: but blessing shall be upon the head of him that selleth it."–Proverbs 11:24-26.

When you give to those that are less fortunate than yourself God sees that and then opens the heavens and pours down financial blessings on you.

"Give, and it shall be given unto you; good measure, pressed down, and shaken together, and running over, shall men give into your bosom. For with the same measure that ye mete withal it shall be measured to you again."–Luke 6:38.

If you are still having a difficult time giving remember that God gave us the greatest gift of all his son Jesus Christ.

Proverbs 19:18

"Chasten thy son while there is hope and let not thy soul spare for his crying."

Train your children early. It is never too soon. Tomorrow may be too late. Do not waste a single day. You do not have forever. Children grow quickly and once they grow beyond training, then they are gone from your influence. When you don't grab the bull by the horns or wait until the horse gets out of the barn to lock up the gate then you have failed. God gave you children when they were needy meaning they were in want of affection, attention, or emotional support. God gave you a window of time to train them, which closes quickly. If you allow that window of time to pass you by then you will require a miracle to have any influence on your children to mold and shape their lives in a godly fashion anymore.

Teaching and chastening your kids is a commandment. "Train up a child in the way he should go: and when he is old, he will not depart from it."–Proverbs 22:6. "And, ye fathers, provoke not your children to wrath: but bring them up in the nurture and admonition of the Lord.–Ephesians 6:4. He that spareth his rod hateth his son: but he that loveth him chasteneth him betimes."– Proverbs 13:24.

A tremendous number of things have changed through the years that are different from what our grandparents and parents encountered. The Ten Commandments has been tossed aside. It is an abomination to have prayer in schools nowadays.

You are not to spank or beat a child to draw blood or damage any part of them. That is considered child abuse. However, chasten your child when necessary. When you really love your children a part of loving them is teaching, correcting, and chastening. So many parents have decided not to chasten their kids and as a result, they are proud, selfish, raucous, disobedient, uncouth, and have numerous other disparaging ways.

Ask God to guide and direct you as a parent and pray daily for your children. One of the best conversations you can have with your children when they are grown and have their own kids is for them to tell you "mom and dad I didn't like it when it was happening but now I am grateful for you being tough and punishing, and spanking me because it has made me a better person and a better parent."

Proverbs 19:24

"A slothful man hideth his hand in his bosom and will not so much as bring it to his mouth again."

Lazy people want everything handed to them. It annoys a lazy person to put forth any effort to do anything. Lazy people will find an excuse for everything and anything. Lazy people have more excuses they spew out of their mouths than days in a year. Programs like Welfare and numerous others allow lazy people to thrive in their situation.

God presented his people with an excellent work ethic where God himself worked six days straight to create this world. Parents you need to teach your children at an early age to clean their rooms, wash the dinner dishes, sweep the floors, vacuum the carpets, take out the garbage, wash their clothes, iron their clothes, walk the dog, remove the clothes from the dryer and fold them up, learn how to cook, etc. This needs to be taught to girls and boys alike especially boys so they don't grow up thinking this is my wife's job.

How many of you have family members still living with you that should have been out on their own a long time ago? How many of you have friends that just keep leeching off you and claim they never have money to pay for a night out? Do you know a co-worker who is always trying to stay away from working and just surf the internet at work all day long or stay on personal phone calls but expects a full paycheck every pay period? Students, who are not popular in school and trying to get friends do you have other students especially athletes that claim they will be your friend if you do their homework for them?

The list is endless of all the situations and circumstances where you will find lazy people. It is up to you to inform them you will not tolerate their laziness and you will not help them reach higher heights in the quest to do nothing. When you stop supporting a lazy person, they have one of two choices. They can either succumb to a life of crime and once they get caught, then they will go straight to jail for their crime which in most cases will be robbery. Or it will force them to get a job, so they can have food to eat and a place to sleep.

Give the gift of gab to a lazy person and tell them to get up and get moving!

Chapter Twenty

Proverbs 20:1

"Wine is a mocker, strong drink is raging: and whosoever is deceived thereby is not wise."

These are words of wisdom. It has destroyed many people's lives and turned them upside down because of the abuse of alcohol. How is it that alcohol and wine make a mockery of people? People partake and indulge in actions they would not do if sober.

Is it wrong to drink wine? No, wine is good. The Lord created wine to cheer people. "And wine that maketh glad the heart of man, and oil to make his face to shine, and bread which strengtheneth man's heart."–Psalms 104:15. It is important that you acknowledge that you must be cautious when drinking.

Overindulging in anything can be detrimental to you. Take exercising for example. Do it but take care how far you go. According to a Forbes Magazine article from June 3, 2018 by contributor Bruce Y Lee the term Rhabdomyolysis is real. If you overwork your muscles and fibers to where it damages your kidney, and it progresses to kidney failure and you ultimately die that was excessive. Even though the odds for this is rare, it is possible and the term for this is Rhabdomyolysis. Just like eating too much will cause you to become overweight and lead to serious health issues drinking too much also has repercussions. When it gets to the level where there are designated driving programs in conjunction with sporting events, we as a people have gone way too far and abused drinking.

The amount of people that have lost their lives to drunk driving is astronomical. Spirits on their own can't cause mischief because they remain bottled until a person pops the cork. "And be not drunk with wine, wherein is excess; but be filled with the Spirit."–Ephesians 5:18.

If your local liquor store opens at 10 am and you are waiting in the parking lot at 9:45, there is a problem, there. If you must keep a flask with you all the times, there is a deep issue here. If you are hiding liquor or wine bottles in your home in the toilet tank so nobody knows you have officially crossed over to the dark side and need to reevaluate how alcohol is controlling, you.

Proverbs 20:9

"Who can say, I have made my heart clean, I am pure from my sin?"

Who do you completely trust? If you answered this question with any answer other than God, you are misleading yourself. Do not say yourself because then you are sadly mistaken. People who don't use wisdom believe in themselves. "For there is not a just man upon earth, that doeth good, and sinneth not." - Ecclesiastes 7:20.

I am sure you have heard of the story of Job in the Bible. "There was a man in the land of Uz, whose name was Job; and that man was perfect and upright, and one that feared God, and eschewed evil."–Job 1:1. Job was blessed in every area of his life but then God allowed Satan to disrupt Job's perfect life. Job lost everything including his health. Now even though Job was perfect he eventually sinned. He sinned because despite his understanding of God Job sinned because he believed the Lord owed him a complete answer as to the reasons for his suffering. Then, after God spoke to Job and revealed that his knowledge as a creature was inadequate to give him the right to question the Almighty's wisdom Job repented of his sin. Then the Bible says God blessed Job much greater in his later years than in his beginning.

Have these things ever happened to you? Your spouse forgets your birthday. They forget to pick up the kids from school. Your friend promises to babysit your children, so you can have a date night with your spouse, but they never show up. Your sibling borrows your car and brings it back empty when they promised to fill up the gas tank. You promise the church you will take part in their next play and will be at every rehearsal, but the big game is on, so you don't go. You promise your mom you will go to the flea market with her but instead; you say you're sick and go to the movies instead. There are numerous scenarios but I'm sure you get my point. There is a very famous wrestler from the WWE named Stone Cold Steve Austin who always said, "Don't Trust Anybody." Well, that includes yourself only trust God!

Proverbs 20:20

"Whoso curseth his father or his mother, his lamp shall be put out in obscure darkness."

How you treat your parents will determine how your life will be. This is a critical piece of wisdom because God listed it as one of the ten commandments he gave to Moses.

Some of you may say you don't know what type of parents I have. They don't deserve to be honored. That may be true but if God says to do it, then just remember the Nike slogan "Just Do It."

God sits high and looks low and is never surprised. He will repay any sinful malice treatment that has been bestowed upon you from your parents. God is the great equalizer. Even better than the esteemed actor Denzel Washington with his equalizer movies. God stated, "Dearly beloved, avenge not yourselves, but rather give place unto wrath: for it is written, Vengeance is mine; I will repay, saith the Lord."–Romans 12:19.

If you want to live a blessed life, honor your parents. Your future will depend upon it. When you curse your parents, you are using obscene or profane words when referring to them or in discussions about them. Some parents did the best they could because they were children when they became parents. Whatever the circumstances maybe you do not have the authority to be judge, jury, and executioner. "And I will execute great vengeance upon them with furious rebukes; and they shall know that I [am] the LORD, when I shall lay my vengeance upon them."–Ezekiel 25:17. "For we know him that hath said, Vengeance [belongeth] unto me, I will recompense, saith the Lord. And again, The Lord shall judge his people."–Hebrews 10:30. "See that none render evil for evil unto any [man]; but ever follow that which is good, both among yourselves, and to all [men]." - 1 Thessalonians 5:15.

Jesus Christ was God's son, but he honored and respected his earthly parents Joseph and Mary. If he can do it, you can too.

Proverbs 20:29

"The glory of young men is their strength: and the beauty of old men is the grey head."

Young men, older men, are both a required asset in today's' society. Young men have an uncanny source of speed, strength, and agility, until their mid-30's. Young men also have impatience, ignorance, and they act foolishly.

Older men have passed that stage in life and now have a vital asset that is called wisdom. They now have full development, knowledge via direct participation, and amass direction. This is depicted by their grey hair.

It is important that all men in these stages of their lives realize they need to respect each other and there is something to be learned from each other. Both men young and old are vital to society.

Older men should admire younger men and what they can do and reflect on what they used to do and no longer can.

Younger men should pay homage to older men just because of their wisdom.

Young men and old men learn to respect and trust each other and use your abilities to service each other.

Book of Proverbs

Chapter Twenty One

Proverbs 21:6

"The getting of treasures by a lying tongue is a vanity tossed to and fro of them that seek death."

Ethics - a set of moral issues or aspects; a guiding philosophy; a consciousness of moral importance.

When you are dealing in trade and management of funds, it requires wisdom. It is very important, to be honest in all business dealings. It is vital you realize that any deceit or fraud will be repaid by God. Any unscrupulous business practices you have done to pad your pockets will ultimately see you lose all the profits you gained.

If you like to lie and falsify your financial dealings beware God sees every crooked deal you do. God will prosper every person you defraud. Even if he must go through 100 people to give back to you what someone took, they will be repaid back what you took from them. God sees every deal you do whether it is legitimate or deceptive and he will give you your just deserts.

God deals in the checks and balances business and he has a log of all your good deeds and all your transgressions.

Have you ever been involved in any of these situations? Is the driver's license you have really yours or did you pay someone to take the test for you? Is the drug test you took really yours with your urine or did you pull a fast one? Is the resume you handed in true or was it fabricated? Do you have a business where you do oil changes on vehicles? If so, did you really put on a new oil filter for the customer? Do you tithe and really give the first tenth of your income to God? Or do you keep it for yourself because you believe the pastor pockets it himself? That is not your concern God will deal with the minister himself. When you are dining out do you tip the server correctly and generously or do you try to get away with the least amount possible? Do you pay your employees on time and the proper amount or do you try to haggle with them on minimal issues?

It does not surprise God, and he sees and knows all things. "Neither is there any creature that is not manifest in his sight: but all things are naked and opened unto the eyes of him with whom we have to do."–Hebrews 4:13.

Always deal honestly, tell the truth, and God will bless you.

Proverbs 21:9

"It is better to dwell in a corner of the housetop, than with a brawling woman in a wide house."

In an online article from news.com.au written by Fiona Macrae back on February 21, 2013, they say women speak 20,000 words per day versus men who only speak 7,000. Scientists have discovered that a higher amount of the Foxp2 protein is the reason women are chattier. Since women have more Foxp2, known as the 'language protein', in their brains they are the chattier of the sexes. Ladies just because there is scientific proof why we talk so much that does not mean we should abuse it.

When we are always talking, harping, complaining, arguing all that does is drive our men away. I went into a Hungry Howie's a while ago to get two salads and I overheard a conversation with a male worker and what appeared to be a woman. I heard him tell the person on the other end of the line "I did not want to have to answer 20,000 questions like I was being questioned by the FBI." I laughed and one of the other workers saw me and I said to him "that guy must be talking to his wife" and he said yes you are correct. When the guy finished his conversation, he walked to the front of the store to get a fountain drink and I smiled, and the other employee said, "even the customer realized you were talking to your wife." The guy tried to smile but was shaking his head at the same time and I said to him, "don't worry all guys go through it. My husband has been dealing with it for 37 years. He laughed, and I took my order and left." Now this story may sound cute and laughable but all women including me are guilty of this and we need to stop.

This is the reason men find other curricular activities to do, or stay late at work, or go into their man cave if they have one so they can get relief from our mouths. If this is the only things, they do you are fortunate but, if they start to not come home after work and they walk away when they get certain phone calls then your mouth has gotten your behind in serious trouble. Ladies, when you get to where there are no more positive affirmation words you speak about and to the man in your life and all you do, is talk, correct, debate, scold, suggest, and remind, the man in your life you are heading in the wrong direction of a one-lane road.

Just like they say for every person who dislikes their job and wants a replacement job that there is somebody who would love to have the job you no longer like or appreciate the same applies to relationships. Car batteries have a negative and positive pole and relationships with the opposite sex are normally the same way. I know you have heard of the book "Men are from Mars Women are from Venus." Truer words were never spoken. However, there is another true statement, "don't wait for the horse to get out of the barn before you lock up the gate." Ladies this means don't antagonize your man so much that he packs his belongings and leaves.

As much as the man in your life may infuriate you think of the times that may come up and he is not there. I realize they make back scratchers but there is nothing like the real thing. Yes, there are many Massage Envy's all over but if you are living paycheck to paycheck, this is not an option if you direly need a massage. If you happen to be blessed with a man that cooks, cleans, vacuums, takes out the garbage, washes dishes, mops the floor, works and earns a living then you learn to deal with all the other irritants. Ok so when he comes home he throws his clothes all over the house, doesn't take the recycle items out every week and now your kitchen is full of items, the cocktail table is full of everything except what should be on the table, he leaves nuts, bolts, screws, and other items in his pants so when you wash the clothes everything except the kitchen sink is falling out of the washing machine. Obviously, the list can be endless but when everything is going the way you like it it's great.

Ladies the most important thing is that you have a man who has a heart for God and when you pick up your left foot to go to church, he picks up his right and you go out the door together.

Proverbs 21:16

"The man that wandereth out of the way of understanding shall remain in the congregation of the dead."

People that wander move about without a fixed course, aim, or goal and appear to be discombobulated. This is not what God desires for his children that is why he has provided us with the Bible as our map. One of the greatest sources of technology nowadays is GPS. I love it. I have no sense of direction and so it is wonderful to just speak an address into my phone and magically directions appear.

Pattern your life according to the teachings in the bible and you will be able to withstand the storms of life that deflate others. "Therefore, whosoever heareth these sayings of mine, and doeth them, I will liken him unto a wise man, which built his house upon a rock: And the rain descended, and the floods came, and the winds blew, and beat upon that house; and it fell not: for it was founded upon a rock. And everyone that heareth these sayings of mine, and doeth them not, shall be likened unto a foolish man, which built his house upon the sand: And the rain descended, and the floods came, and the winds blew, and beat upon that house; and it fell: and great was the fall of it."–Matthew 7:24-27.

People have been trying forever to do things their way instead of God's way. When Moses went up into the mountain to be with

God the children of Israel built a molten calf and made that their God and worshiped that. When Moses returned with the tablets of the Ten Commandments, he threw them down at the calf and destroyed it. The people thought Moses was dead and so they created and built themselves a leader. All sin starts with just one wrong thought.

Humble yourself and remember you did not create yourself God did and so wander in his direction. I love the song and the artist. There will never be another Frank Sinatra, but we all need to stop the "My Way" attitude and do it God's way.

Chapter Twenty Two

Proverbs 22:4

"By humility and the fear of the Lord are riches, and honour, and life."

Humble yourself before your Creator, and you will have unlimited blessings heaped upon you. Since we as people think so highly of ourselves it is difficult to reverse that thought process and think lowly of ourselves.

Humility is the first part of this proverb. A humble person admits they are a sinner, they don't know everything, and that you cannot accomplish anything without God's help. People who have this wisdom are quick to say they are sorry, so no escalations arise. They are just like Jesus they are servers. Remember how Jesus washed the disciple's feet. They are not loud and haughty and make a big to do about themselves. They realize they are to praise and uplift others.

The second part of this proverb refers to having the fear of the Lord. A person who fears the Lord does not want to grieve him. This is the same as willingly and knowingly having an extramarital affair and your spouse finds out and the hurt you cause them. When you love someone, you try to do everything to please them.

"When a man's ways please the Lord, he maketh even his enemies to be at peace with him."–Proverbs 16:7.

Riches are one way in which God will bless you. Remember Solomon asked God for wisdom and humbled himself and God blessed him with incredible wealth.

A humble person God honors. For every person who is humble and reserved God will promote and magnify before men.

"Humble yourselves therefore under the mighty hand of God that he may exalt you in due time: Casting all your care upon him; for he careth for you."–1 Peter 5:6-7.

Proverbs 22:7

"The rich ruleth over the poor, and the borrower is servant to the lender."

Money gives you power and leverage but don't be deceived because money also corrupts a person. Those with no wisdom having lots of money can lead you into temptation and dangerous situations.

Most people have credit cards, and they can be helpful; however, they should not be misused as this can and will cause great distress. Constant phone calls around the clock from lenders when you don't pay on time, the looming possibility of debt consolidation, and the big monster filing for bankruptcy.

There is a huge difference between a need and a want. A need is a condition requiring supply or relief, or a lack of the means of subsistence. A want is to have a strong desire for something.

Unfortunately, this is the category many people fall into when they have excessive credit card debt. There is a difference from needing to purchase diapers for your infant newborn as opposed to wanting to purchase the new sofa and love sets so you can impress your friends. If you need to impress and get friends this way, then they are the wrong set of people from the beginning and stay clear. Fake false people will eventually show their true colors.

Life happens and sometimes things go wrong but making a habit of it is not the godly way. You can work for a well-established firm for multiple years and after being in your home for many years you have an extension put on the home and the home next door is for sale and you decide to purchase it and expand your home and next thing you know you walk into work on Monday and are advised the firm is closing down immediately. That news is devastating but remember it does not surprise God. If God got you that job, he will get you another one. Let go and let God.

Once he picks you up and you are on course again, you must be mindful not to allow yourself to become the tail again and wind up being the servant to the lender.

Proverbs 22:9

"He that hath a bountiful eye shall be blessed; for he giveth of his bread to the poor."

Are you a generous person? If you, are you have and will be blessed? God loves a cheerful giver. Do you get excited when opportunities arise where you can give to help others? Or are you the opposite where you want to hold on to every penny you have and frown at helping others? Are you more like the Grinch but instead of just Christmas time you are like that all year round? If you are, it disappoints God. You will never become all you are and meant to be.

God loves generous givers. Do you give to the poor? "Blessed is he that considereth the poor: the Lord will deliver him in time of trouble. The Lord will preserve him and keep him alive; and he shall be blessed upon the earth: and thou wilt not deliver him unto the will of his enemies. The Lord will strengthen him upon the bed of languishing: thou wilt make all his bed in his sickness."–Psalms 41:1-3.

Who is it you can bless and give to today? There are so many opportunities to give every day. Who has a legitimate need? God sits high and looks low and sees what you do with what he has blessed you with. Don't wait until you have hundreds or thousands of dollars to give. Give from the place where you are, and God will bless you. Compassion and love are traits of a godly person. "The liberal soul shall be made fat: and he that watereth shall be watered also himself."–Proverbs 11:25. "Now unto him that is able to do exceeding abundantly above all that we ask or think, according to the power that worketh in us, unto him be glory in the church by Christ Jesus throughout all ages, world without end. Amen."–Ephesians 3:20-21.

Who can you truly assist? Think hard. Giving and helping those in need should always be at the top of your thought process. God has not been withholding or stingy with you so why are you with others? Giving to the poor and helping others gets you more financial deposits in God's bank. No one will ever be able to out-give God so give, give, give and see God bless you with the triple crown win.

Proverbs 22:17

"Bow down thine ear, and hear the words of the wise, and apply thine heart unto my knowledge."

This proverb has three separate parts that if you apply them will lead you to truth and wisdom. You must learn humility, you need to use your ears more and hear and listen and stop talking so much, and finally, you must apply the knowledge you will be taught.

Naturally, people don't like these three things and so they never reach the heights that God has ordained for them. The first part of this proverb refers to bowing down your ear. Now anyone who bows down to something is humbling themselves. However, most of us think more of ourselves than we should and so this is a difficult task for us to master. "For I say, through the grace given unto me, to every man that is among you, not to think of himself more highly than he ought to think; but to think soberly, according as God hath dealt to every man the measure of faith."–Romans 12:3. To humble yourself, you must get rid of pride. You are not to think of yourself as incapable of doing anything or minimizing your talents. You must remember who provided you with those talents and give God the praise, honor, and glory for giving you what you have.

The second part of these proverbs discusses hearing the words of the wise. If you want to hear anything you must stop talking. We as people are always too busy doing things. We always need to have something going on all the time. I am guilty of that as well because unlike some authors I write with music or sometimes even the TV playing. That works for me. However, there must come a time when we need to get quiet and learn and receive. If you are presented with an opportunity to get around older people who are talking grab a seat and listen. For example, at family reunions. The older grey headed people have wisdom and knowledge, and you can learn a lot from them. Stop texting on your phone and breathe in the knowledge when and while you can. Nowadays almost everywhere you go you are being told to silence your cell phones, don't text, and stop talking. This is something they say before the start of every movie you see. It is really a shame they say that in churches as well. I mean come on you are there to hear the word of God everything else can wait!

Finally, the third part of this proverb discusses applying your heart. Everything in life is a choice and you must choose to change your ways and expand your knowledge and horizons to crave wisdom and knowledge. It is your choice to learn and love wisdom and knowledge and reject everything contrary to them.

Children listen to your parents because they have lived longer than you and know more. Adults listen to someone who has proven they have wisdom. Since many people think about things on a financial level, then mull this over. If you were to come into a large sum of money, would you listen to advice from your good friend who earns less income than you do and is constantly broke and trying to hit you up for money whenever they can or would you seek the advice of a financial advisor before you make one wrong move and lose everything? This is one of the greatest goals you can achieve if you can humble yourself, learn to listen and stop talking all the time and apply your heart.

Book of Proverbs

Chapter Twenty Three

Proverbs 23:4

"Labour not to be rich: cease from thine own wisdom."

Your main goal in life should be to be successful at being a godly person and to do what pleases God. When you do these things God will bless everything else including your business dealings and finances. Unfortunately, society has that twisted around. Society tells you to trust in yourself and labor to do what you believe will bring you tremendous wealth. Let me remind you whatever you have here on earth will not follow you when you die. You can make many deals with the funeral home but if they don't cheat you out of it your family will just because of greed. The bottom line is you can own a multitude of homes and properties, but they cannot go with you. One of the greatest entertainers this world has ever seen had a tremendous home he called Neverland Ranch. When Michael Jackson died in 2009, he could not take this property with him. "For we brought nothing into this world, and it is certain we can carry nothing out."–1 Timothy 6:7.

There is an old saying that people with wisdom and grey hair always said. "Your eye is bigger than your belly." What this means is that you put too much food on your plate and once you eat you cannot finish it. This is something that is so prevalent in the United States where so much food gets wasted. People's greedy nature just always desire more. If you have one or two homes maybe one is a vacation home if you are not into time-shares, then why do you need multiple homes especially if you cannot manage them? If you are someone with finances like Oprah Winfrey that is a different story. Oprah can own, manage, and handle multiple dwellings and part of the reason she is so blessed is that she is generous. Remember, we spoke about giving generously in chapter 22.

Having money and wealth is not the problem it is the love of money that is the root of all evil. "For the love of money is the root of all evil: which while some coveted after, they have erred from the faith, and pierced themselves through with many sorrows."–1 Timothy 6:10.

Focus on God and pray for wisdom and to know your purpose in life that God has ordained for you. That will flourish all the extras upon you by your heavenly father.

Proverbs 23:5

"Wilt thou set thine eyes upon that which is not? for riches certainly make themselves wings; they fly away as an eagle toward heaven."

Harry Houdini, Dynamo, David Copperfield, Penn & Teller, David Blaine, Harry Blackstone Jr, Criss Angel, Harry August Jansen, Derren Brown, Ricky Jay, Michael Carbonaro and countless other are great magicians and illusionists. When a person spends his entire life trying to get wealth and riches and believes, they will be with him forever that is an illusion.

"And he spake a parable unto them, saying, the ground of a certain rich man brought forth plentifully: And he thought within himself, saying, what shall I do, because I have no room where to bestow my fruits? And he said, this will I do: I will pull down my barns and build greater; and there will I bestow all my fruits and my goods. And I will say to my soul, Soul, thou hast much goods laid up for many years; take thine ease, eat, drink, and be merry. But God said unto him, thou fool, this night thy soul shall be required of thee: then whose shall those things be, which thou hast provided? So is he that layeth up treasure for himself and is not rich toward God."–Luke 12:16-21.

We all arrived naked into this world and naked we shall return. "And said, Naked came I out of my mother's womb, and naked shall I return thither: the Lord gave, and the Lord hath taken away; blessed be the name of the Lord."–Job 1:21.

Consider this the more you make or the greater your wealth the more you pay. When you do your taxes the more you earned for the year the greater the tax you will need to repay. For many years the New York Yankees had tremendous baseball teams and have won 27 World Series. Now let me pause here for a moment I am not a New York Yankees fan however my husband is, but that is a story for another time. People would always say the Yankees were buying players to win championships. Whether that was true or not what was a fact is that they had to pay extra. They put the luxury tax in place of a salary cap to level the spending an individual team can spend on their roster. The New York Yankees were over the threshold from 2003 to 17, paying $341 million.

Remember the Lord's warning, "Lay not up for yourselves treasures upon earth, where moth and rust doth corrupt, and where thieves break through and steal: But lay up for yourselves treasures in heaven, where neither moth nor rust doth corrupt, and where thieves do not break through nor steal: For where your treasure is, there will your heart be also."–Matthew 6:19-21.

Proverbs 23:12

"Apply thine heart unto instruction, and thine ears to the words of knowledge."

Every day, we are given multiple opportunities to make choices. If we make them using wisdom and they work out, then we are considered wise. If we make them careless and haphazardly, then we are considered foolish.

Do you know how many minutes per day you could improve your life by seeking wisdom? How much of that time do you seek wisdom? Do you read your bible? Do you seek people who have shown themselves to be wise? How many of these minutes do you pursue knowledge? Do you read a portion of a book that teaches wisdom and provides instruction and insight every day?

Entertainment and fun are great, but you will never become all God designed you to be if all you do is entertain yourself. "There is nothing better for a man, than that he should eat and drink, and that he should make his soul enjoy good in his labour. This also I saw that it was from the hand of God."–Ecclesiastes 2:24. "And also that every man should eat and drink, and enjoy the good of all his labour, it is the gift of God." Ecclesiastes 3:13. There are many ways we can entertain ourselves, but we also need to apply time to increase our wisdom, knowledge, and understanding and spend time with God. Now the following categories of people are busy, but they still find time for God. If, these are ways you earn a living, then your time is more limited. I don't mean if you are an NFL, MLB, NHL, NBA, Tennis, Golf, Figure Skater, Soccer player or other sports. Nor am I referring to if you are, for example, a baseball scout. Then this is your job and you must spend a lot of time engaging in it mentally and physically traveling around from state to state and city to city. Sometimes even a different country if you must be in Canada. However, if not you need to engage yourself in things that please God and gaining wisdom and knowledge you can pass down to the next generation.

Proverbs 23:23

"Buy the truth, and sell it not; also wisdom, and instruction, and understanding."

"And remember, never let those ruby slippers off your feet for a moment, or you will be at the mercy of the Wicked Witch of the West." This is a quote from the classic movie "The Wizard of Oz" with Judy Garland. The same way it was crucial that she never take off the ruby slippers is the same way you should never allow yourself to be without truth, wisdom, instruction, and understanding.

The truth will cost you, friends, because some people believe in saying and doing what will benefit them. Have you ever heard the saying, "tell the truth and shame the devil?" It's like Judge Judy says, "If you tell the truth, you don't have to have a good memory. If you lie, you're always tripping over your own tie."

Wisdom will cost you comfort because when people live life foolishly, they do whatever they please. When you apply wisdom, then you have great insight and good judgment. An example of not using wisdom would be to express negative thoughts about your boss in the presence of other employees especially ones you know don't like you.

Instruction will cost you to become humble and give up your prideful ways. When you accept instructions that tells the world you don't know everything, and you need help and guidance.

Finally, understanding will cost you peace of mind. When you realize the extreme folly of this world, then you know you have gained something special.

The Book of Proverbs was created to guide and direct you but you will not get the full value of it unless you read and study it. They designed it to read daily that is why there are 31 chapters. Read and re-read and ask God to enlighten each verse so you can master truth, wisdom, instruction, and understanding.

Chapter Twenty Four

Proverbs 24:10

"If thou faint in the day of adversity, thy strength is small."

"I'm convinced that about half of what separates the successful entrepreneurs from the non-successful ones is pure perseverance."–Steve Jobs

Are you a persistent person? Are you a never say die person? Are you a determined person? If you are that person then you are familiar with this bible verse, "I can do all things through Christ which strengtheneth me."–Philippians 4:13.

However, if you are the person who gets frustrated often, gives up easily, has a negative mindset, then you are weak. If you are this person, then you know this bible verse well, "The slothful man saith, there is a lion without, I shall be slain in the streets."–Proverbs 22:13.

No person likes adversity, difficult situations, painful experiences, but these are the things that will strengthen you. This is how God measures your faith in him. God will allow trouble, trials, and difficulties to come your way just to see how much faith you have and how much you rely on him instead of yourself.

It is a lie to believe you can live a life for Christ that has no trials or adversity. There are countless men in the Bible who had to endure afflictions like Job, Moses, David, or Paul. "Many are the afflictions of the righteous: but the Lord delivereth him out of them all."–Psalm 34:19.

Adversity strengthens your faith. Faith cannot be built by prosperity, but by adversity. If everything was always going well for you, there would be no need to have faith. If every day was so perfect like you were lying in a hammock under a palm tree with a beautiful sunny day and a light breeze in Maui Hawaii swinging from side to side in the hammock then why would you need to rely on God? If you were a race car driver, and you did 100 laps on the track with no other cars or competition but after you finished then the race started again and instead of just you they added 29 other cars and you had to work harder to get the win which race would emphasize your stamina, resolve, diligence where they should present you with the racing trophy?

"Success consists of going from failure to failure without the loss of enthusiasm."–Winston Churchill. "If you're going through hell, keep going."–Winston Churchill. "Success is not final, failure is not fatal: it is the courage to continue that counts."–Winston Churchill. "A pessimist sees the difficulty in every opportunity; an optimist sees the opportunity in every difficulty."–Winston Churchill.

Which one are you? How great are you? How strong are you?

Proverbs 24:12

"If thou sayest, Behold, we knew it not; doth not he that pondereth the heart consider it? and he that keepeth thy soul, doth not he know it? and shall not he render to every man according to his works?"

As a child of God, you cannot live behind the veil like a veil with a wedding dress. In life, you must step out and make yourself known to be visible. If you know that something wrong is taking place you need to get involved. We are here to help each other not just for our own personal comfort or gain.

A great number of people refuse to get out of their comfort zone. They hope and rely on the fact that others will take care of a problem. Many people dislike getting involved because it may cost them money or time. They figure if they ignore things happening around them that's their prerogative however that is untrue. God sees and hears everything and will judge you accordingly.

If you live next door to a couple where you have witnessed the man physically abusing the woman and then the unthinkable happens where the woman gets killed and the cops come to your home to question you and you say you never heard or saw anything just to not get involved you may get away with the lie to the cops but God is sitting up in heaven and shaking his head. You cannot deceive God.

The person in the above example chose and pretended not to know. This is no excuse for not getting involved to save a life.

There is a new campaign with homeland security called, "If you see something say something." It is important that we look out for each other because we would want someone to do the same for us.

Proverbs 24:16

"For a just man falleth seven times, and riseth up again: but the wicked shall fall into mischief."

God never intended life to be wine and roses for us. Why should he? He even had his son Jesus Christ suffer the unimaginable by being nailed to the cross for our sins. Remember Jesus was sin free when he went to the cross for all our atrocities.

Numerous people in the bible were challenged with adversity because they followed God, and because they did God made them prevail. The most well-recognized ones were David and Paul.

David was a man after God's heart but at times seemed like he was a dual personality like Dr. Jekyll and Mr. Hyde. David was one character in the bible that committed some of the greatest infractions. David engaged in adultery with Batsheba and then orchestrated the murder of her husband Uriah.

Paul who was first called Saul who was a Jew went around persecuting Christians. Eventually, he converted and followed God after Jesus confronted him while traveling from Jerusalem to Damascus. We recognize Paul as writing 13 of the 27 books in the New Testament. Paul had many tribulations and was persecuted numerous times and fell short repeatedly, but God continued to walk with him and lift him up again and again.

There is no reason to get agitated or concerned when you have transgressed. Just trust God and he will raise you up in due season.

Proverbs 24:29

"Say not, I will do so to him as he hath done to me: I will render to the man according to his work."

Forgiveness, letting go of grudges, bitterness, and not planning revenge. When you forgive someone, you are giving them amnesty or pardoning them. Sounds so princely and glorious right? This requires daily work. Trust me, I know. This has probably been one of my greatest battles. Women have long memories and tend to not give up or give in easily. However, that is not the way in which God wants us to be.

I remember when someone said if you remember another's offense against you, then he or she becomes your master. Well, I used to think it is silly until I saw what they meant. When the mere mention of someone's name causes the hair on your back to raise up, when you find it difficult to sleep because you keep reflecting on what this person did to you, when you are going somewhere and you know that person will be there and you plot what you can say to hurt them or do where you can avenge what they did to you then they have become your master.

If you believe if you don't get revenge for what someone did to you, then you have forgotten that God is your first line of defense. "Dearly beloved, avenge not yourselves, but rather give place unto wrath: for it is written, Vengeance is mine; I will repay, saith the Lord. Therefore, if thine enemy hunger, feed him; if he thirst, give him drink: for in so doing thou shalt heap coals of fire on his head. Be not overcome of evil but overcome evil with good."– Romans 12:19-21.

I know I have mentioned this previously but because forgiveness is so important and a sermon that is preached in churches so often because so many of us have difficulties with it one of the greatest examples of forgiveness you can see is in the film "Unbroken: Path To Redemption." They released it in the movies back in 2018. It is now available on DVD. You should get a copy and watch it from time to time to help you if you are a person that has difficulties forgiving people that have hurt you.

Remember the golden rule, "Do unto others as you would have them do unto you." All of us know sometimes we have treated someone unjustly and wish we could take back what we said or how we treated that person. If you want them to forgive you, then you must do the same.

Chapter Twenty Five

Proverbs 25:11

"A word fitly spoken is like apples of gold in pictures of silver."

How does color make you feel? They say color excites the senses. They call another name for the Autumn season Fall. Down here in Florida most people love when fall starts because they can cool down some from the 90 to 100-degree temperatures. Fall is when the leaves change in color and they look beautiful. You see some of the most magnificent colors like red, yellow, purple, black, orange, pink, magenta, blue and brown.

One of the greatest painters ever was Vincent Van Gogh. His work included landscapes, still bold colors and dramatic, impulsive and expressive brushwork characterized life's, portraits and self-portraits.

There is an artist named Dale Chihuly who is a glass sculptor. Words cannot describe this man's talents, vision, and imagination. It is truly inspiring. His use of color is amazing. I first found out about him and saw one of his exhibits in Seattle WA July 2017. I am looking forward to going to the Morean Art Center in St. Petersburg FL to see another of his exhibits. What makes his colorful work so amazing is that in 1976, while Chihuly was in

England, he was involved in a head-on car accident during which he flew through the windshield. Glass severely cut his face and it blinded him in his left eye. If you have never seen his work, look him up online or plan a trip to one of his many galleries.

The same way in which color can excite your senses it is the same way when you speak kind words to people. It brings a smile to their face; it uplifts them inside. Try it sometimes. While the cashier is checking you out in the grocery store ask them how is their day? How are they feeling? Thank them for their service and see how happy they get. We never know what a person may be going through, and you may be the one to lift their spirits.

How excellent is your speech? Is it like apples of gold in pictures of silver? If not, become the beacon of light in someone's life. Speak color into their life that will excite their senses and uplift them.

Proverbs 25:19

"Confidence in an unfaithful man in time of trouble is like a broken tooth, and a foot out of joint."

Are you a faithful person? Do you fulfill your commitments? Do you associate yourself with people that are faithful? If not, this proverb is talking directly to you.

One of the most consistent exercise machines through the years is the Treadmill. It provides a fantastic cardiovascular workout and enhances your heart health. Whether walking or running on the treadmill it will keep a continuous flow of blood pumping to your heart and lower the stress on your heart.

There are women that say having a toothache is worse than giving birth. One thing for sure both are painful. Are you blessed to have faithful friends? If so, then you should treasure them. True friends are a great blessing and they prove that when you run into trials and tribulations. There remain grounded and are there for you any time of the day or night.

True faithful friends symbolize the saying "when the going gets tough the tough gets going." However, if when you really need them, they are running in the opposite direction they are not faithful friends. They are leeches just around when things are good and looking for you to take care of them.

Look for people that love, trust, and fear God. People that follow God's commandments are people you should have as friends you can trust will be there when you need them. Remember how Peter denied Jesus three times.

There is only one faithful friend for any person and that is the Lord Himself! God will always be there for you. "When my father and my mother forsake me, then the Lord will take me up."–Psalm 27:10. "God is our refuge and strength, a very present help in trouble. Therefore, will not we fear, though the earth be removed, and though the mountains be carried into the midst of the sea; Though the waters thereof roar and be troubled, though the mountains shake with the swelling thereof. Selah. There is a river, the streams whereof shall make glad the city of God, the holy place of the tabernacles of the most high. God is in the midst of her; she shall not be moved: God shall help her, and that right early. The heathen raged, the kingdoms were moved: he uttered his voice, the earth melted. The Lord of hosts is with us; the God of Jacob is our refuge. Selah. Come, behold the works of the Lord, what desolations he hath made in the earth. He maketh wars to cease unto the end of the earth; he breaketh the bow, and cutteth the spear in sunder; he burneth the chariot in the fire. Be still and know that I am God: I will be exalted among the heathen, I will be exalted in the earth. The Lord of hosts is with us; the God of Jacob is our refuge. Selah."–Psalm 46.

Proverbs 25:21-22

"If thine enemy be hungry, give him bread to eat; and if he be thirsty, give him water to drink: For thou shalt heap coals of fire upon his head, and the Lord shall reward thee."

Do you love your enemies? Do you treat them the same as you treat your friends? People naturally want to limit love to those that love them and are in their inner circle. Anyone outside of this circle gets the boot just like a horse kicking up his back legs and people go flying in the air.

Jesus says love your enemies. The way you love your enemies is by treating them well despite what they have done to you. Now obviously this is not something that will come easily for the natural man. Now, why should you do this? Because you love God and that is what he commands us to do. The blessing of God is upon those who return blessings for hurt. Is it easy? Nothing new is simple or easy it must be acquired and worked at. They say caviar is an acquired taste. When you are first doing something new, they say it takes 30 days for it to become a habit second nature to you. Besides, it's so comical to do good to those who mistreat you and when you look back in their direction, you see the quizzical look on their face.

"But I say unto you, love your enemies, bless them that curse you, do good to them that hate you, and pray for them which despitefully use you, and persecute you; that ye may be the children of your Father which is in heaven: for he maketh his sun to rise on the evil and on the good, and sendeth rain on the just and on the unjust."–Matthew 5:44-45.

Have you ever heard of the story of the good Samaritan? The Good Samaritan showed great kindness to a racial and religious enemy a Jewish person. "And Jesus answering said, A certain man went down from Jerusalem to Jericho, and fell among thieves, which stripped him of his raiment, and wounded him, and departed, leaving him half dead. And by chance there came down a certain priest that way: and when he saw him, he passed by on the other side. And likewise, a Levite, when he was at the place, came and looked on him, and passed by on the other side. But a certain Samaritan, as he journeyed, came where he was: and when he saw him, he had compassion on him, and went to him, and bound up his wounds, pouring in oil and wine, and set him on his own beast, and brought him to an inn, and took care of him. And on the morrow when he departed, he took out two pence, and gave them to the host, and said unto him, take care of him; and whatsoever thou spendest more, when I come again, I will repay thee. Which now of these three, thinkest thou, was neighbour unto him that fell among the thieves? And he said, He that shewed mercy on him. Then said Jesus unto him, Go, and do thou likewise."–Luke 10:30-37.

God will reward the man and woman who treats his personal enemies with kindness. Even though an enemy's persecution is painful, the Lord will bless you.

Book of Proverbs

Chapter Twenty Six

Proverbs 26:4

"Answer not a fool according to his folly, lest thou also be like unto him."

Time is precious so do not waste it on fools. Truth and wisdom will be lost on fools. If you argue wisdom and truth with a foolish person, they will look down on you with contempt and mock the cherished words you will try to enlighten them with.

Jesus tells us, "Give not that which is holy unto the dogs, neither cast ye your pearls before swine, lest they trample them under their feet, and turn again and rend you."–Matthew 7:6. This may sound harsh, but it is true.

When do you know you have encountered a fool? "Go from the presence of a foolish man, when thou perceivest not in him the lips of knowledge."–Proverbs 14:7. It is easy like the word says just allow them to speak and you will know. Fools believe in themselves only. What they say matters, they trust only their ideas, they believe only they can instruct and teach others, they enjoy disparaging people but most important they don't believe the Bible and the wisdom it offers.

The natural man always wants to get in the last word but when you are dealing with a fool, you will never get them to see things your way so stop trying. Stay grounded in the word and rise above the urge to debate with a fool so you don't wind up sinking to their level and become a fool just like them.

Proverbs 26:11

"As a dog returneth to his vomit, so a fool returneth to his folly."

They say a dog is a man's best friend. Having a dog has lots of positive benefits. Stroking and petting your dog helps to keep your blood pressure low. Owning a dog makes you a social butterfly. Having a dog keeps you active and helps you lose weight because of walking the dog. Owning a dog enhances your health.

With the list of all the benefits of having a dog offers there is always a negative. We have all sometime or another witnessed a dog going back to eat his own vomit. It is gross. Take the mental picture you have in your mind now and replace that dog with a foolish person.

What sinful follies have you rejected? What types of vomit are you tempted to return to? Overeating, drunkenness, drugs, adultery, pornography unforgiveness? You must place a protective shield around yourself and stay away from things that will tempt you to return to your vomit. If it is overeating don't go to buffets. If it is drunkenness, don't allow alcohol in your home and even if you go out of your way driving, go a different direction from where a liquor store is. Don't keep company with people who do drugs. If it is adultery, don't take a second look at a good-looking person who raises sparks within you. If its pornography then place a block on your tablet, a phone, a computer for all those types of sites which can tempt you. If it is unforgiveness keep a book by your bedside that teaches you why unforgiveness is unhealthy. They say one thing highly successful people do before they go to bed is to focus on the positive. If you are reading a book about becoming a forgiving person that is positive.

Pray and ask God to help you stay away from foolish ways and to steer clear of returning to your vomit.

Proverbs 26:20

"Where no wood is, there the fire goeth out: so where there is no talebearer, the strife ceaseth."

How many times has someone said this to you, "can I trust you not to say anything to a certain person? Can you keep a secret?" A godly person should immediately say no thank you. I don't want to know. However, the natural man always peeks with these types of invitations and next thing you know you wind up telling another person what you shouldn't have said or worst you say to the exact person what you should not have said.

Gossip is telling negative information about someone. To the people who engage in this, it doesn't matter whether the information is true.

Talebearing has become so rampant nowadays there are countless magazines that embellish this thing. God does not approve of talebearing. "A naughty person, a wicked man, walketh with a froward mouth". –Proverbs 6:12. Gossip causes enormous pain for people.

Do you care enough about others to stave off talking about them in a disparaging way? If you talk a lot, you probably perpetrate this sin. Ask the Holy Spirit to show you every time you engage in this behavior. Since many of us think so much about finances get yourself a piggy bank or large jar and every time you engage in this folly, you put a dollar in the jar. It will amaze you in 30 days how the jar has filled up. Don't be hard on yourself because we are all guilty of this folly. When God sees you are working towards improvement, he will bless you.

Proverbs 26:27

"Whoso diggeth a pit shall fall therein: and he that rolleth a stone, it will return upon him."

When you dig a ditch, you better dig two because the trap you set may just be for you. What goes around comes around.

I am sure you have heard of the animated cartoon, Tom and Jerry. It revolved on a rivalry between its two title characters, Tom, a cat, and Jerry, a mouse. The shows usually centered on Tom's many attempts to capture Jerry. Tom rarely catches Jerry, mainly because of Jerry's cleverness, cunning abilities, and luck. A lot of times Tom got trapped in the same devices he set to catch Jerry.

Wicked men devise traps and trouble for the innocent and righteous as you can see with what Tom tried countless times to do to Jerry. Do you have enemies? Do you have evil people that are trying to destroy you? Fear not because God will avenge every wrong that has been done to you. "Dearly beloved, avenge not yourselves, but rather give place unto wrath: for it is written, Vengeance is mine; I will repay, saith the Lord."–Romans 12:19. "He made a pit, and digged it, and is fallen into the ditch which he made. His mischief shall return upon his own head, and his violent dealing shall come down upon his own pate."–Psalms 7:15-16.

Let go and let God. The God of glory does not slumber or sleep. Every time the wicked conspire against you, God will turn their devices on their own heads.

Book of Proverbs

Chapter Twenty Seven

Proverbs 27:1

"Boast not thyself of tomorrow; for thou knowest not what a day may bring forth."

"This is the day which the Lord hath made; we will rejoice and be glad in it."–Psalms 118:24. Today is today not tomorrow or next week or next month, not even next year. God gives us grace one day at a time. God gives us grace for today, grace for what's right in front of us. God has given us the supply of grace we need for navigating today and today only. God's grace is like manna. God gives us a day's portion every day.

Living one day at a time is so important that they have titled songs and a TV show from many years ago with that name. God does not provide us with a crystal ball for our lives. Sure, sometimes we should think ahead like when we are planning a vacation, planning a wedding, planning for retirement, etc. However, when you plan these things, be sure to add "If the Lord will." However, we should focus mainly on taking one day at a time. "Go to now, ye that say, today or tomorrow we will go into such a city, and continue there a year, and buy and sell, and get gain: whereas ye know not what shall be on the morrow. For what is your life? It is even a vapour, that appeareth for a little time, and then vanisheth away. For that ye ought to say, if the Lord will, we shall live, and do this, or that. But now ye rejoice in your boastings: all such rejoicing is evil."–James 4:13-16.

We were created to take one day at a time and to praise and worship God. "This people have I formed for myself; they shall shew forth my praise."–Isaiah 43:21. "Let everything that hath breath praise the Lord. Praise ye the Lord."–Psalm 150:6. "Praise ye the Lord. Praise, O ye servants of the Lord, praise the name of the Lord. Blessed be the name of the Lord from this time forth and for evermore. From, the rising of the sun unto the going down of the same the Lord's name is to be praised."- Psalm 113:1-3. "Therefore, I say unto you, take no thought for your life, what ye shall eat, or what ye shall drink; nor yet for your body, what ye shall put on. Is not the life more than meat, and the body than raiment? Behold the fowls of the air: for they sow not, neither do they reap, nor gather into barns; yet your heavenly Father feedeth them. Are ye not much better than they? Which of you by taking thought can add one cubit unto his stature? And why take ye thought for raiment? Consider the lilies of the field, how they grow; they toil not, neither do they spin: And yet I say unto you, that even Solomon in all his glory was not arrayed like one of these. Wherefore, if God so clothe the grass of the field which today is, and tomorrow is cast into the oven, shall he not much more clothe you, O ye of little faith? Therefore, take no thought, saying, what shall we eat? or, what shall we drink? or, Wherewithal shall we be clothed? For, after all these things do the Gentiles seek:) for your heavenly Father knoweth that ye have need of all these things. But seek ye first the kingdom of God, and his righteousness; and all these things shall be added unto you.

Take therefore no thought for the morrow: for the morrow shall take thought for the things of itself. Sufficient unto the day is the evil thereof."–Matthew 6:25-34.

Daily we should all proclaim "Thank God for Life" especially since the next minute isn't promised to us. Things can change from minute to minute. Here in Florida one minute it can be what they call the state "The Sunshine State" but in another minute the clouds above can grow dark and it pours rain. You should live one day at a time. You should count each day a gift and use it wisely to God's glory.

Proverbs 27:2

"Let another man praise thee, and not thine own mouth; a stranger, and not thine own lips."

"O generation of vipers, how can ye, being evil, speak good things? for, out of the abundance of the heart the mouth speaketh."–Matthew 12:34.

The word "I" places you in a category that does not please God. When you speak about yourself too much that means you are not a humble person and your ears are pleased to hear you always talking about yourself. Gaining merit and receiving commendation from people is one thing but trying to get it by praising yourself is disgusting.

Gracious people don't believe in self-praise or boasting. When you don't seek your own praise and glory but are more interested in the things of others God is pleased. "Charity suffereth long and is kind; charity envieth not; charity vaunteth not itself, is not puffed up, Doth not behave itself unseemly, seeketh not her own, is not easily provoked, thinketh no evil; Rejoiceth not in iniquity, but rejoiceth in the truth; Beareth all things, believeth all things, hopeth all things, endureth all things."–1 Corinthians 13:4-7.

When you must discuss your accomplishments to a prospective employer be truthful and speak about your accolades. This is when you want to shine.

Model your life in the same fashion that Jesus did when he was here on earth. His life was dedicated to the service of God and others.

Proverbs 27:20

"Hell and destruction are never full; so the eyes of man are never satisfied."

King Solomon likens the insatiable nature of death and destruction to the insatiable nature of the eyes of man. It does not satisfy both. The lust of the eyes is one of the world's ways of drawing you away from the Lord. "Love not the world, neither the things that are in the world. If any man love the world, the love of the Father is not in him. For all that is in the world, the lust of the flesh, and the lust of the eyes, and the pride of life, is not of the Father, but is of the world."–1 John 2:15-16.

There is no place in the Bible where it says, Stop! Hell is full. So, because of that people never say, I've had enough. I have everything I need. We as sons and daughters of the Living God need to learn to be happy with what we have and to focus on only

156

what we need. "But godliness with contentment is great gain."–1 Timothy 6:6.

Foolish people are preposterous. When a person's desires are so insatiable there is no end no matter what it is. Whether that is money, real estate properties, boats, cars, businesses, sex, drugs and whatever else drives them. Unfortunately, therefore divorce courts are always full, there are so many places to attend Alcohol Anonymous meetings, and why there is never an empty prison around and they are looking to build more.

This started from the beginning of time with Adam and Eve who had everything but wasn't satisfied. "And when the woman saw that the tree was good for food and that it was pleasant to the eyes, and a tree to be desired to make one wise, she took of the fruit thereof, and did eat, and gave also unto her husband with her; and he did eat."–Genesis 3:6. Adam and Eve were not content in Paradise, and because of their discontent, they paid a high price that the world will continue to pay until Jesus Christ returns.

Ladies duplicating Imelda Marcos closet of shoes is unnecessary. You can only wear one pair at a time and most likely there are several pairs that you have purchased that you will never wear.

Gentlemen it is unnecessary to have so many tools you can sell them back to Home Depot, Lowe's, and Harbor Freight. There is no need for 42 Flathead Screwdrivers, 67 Phillips Screwdrivers, 19 Crescent Wrenches, 27 Socket Wrenches, 16 Vise Grip Plyers, 11 Needle Nose Plyers, 18 Hammers, etc. These numbers are just examples. You guys get my point. Unless you own a repair shop which if you do, they belong in your place of business and not in the garage you have attached to your home. Trust me, I've been there, done that, know what it's all about. My husband and I owned a home in Queens when we lived in New York. It was a small two-story single home, but it was on ¼ acre of land. Now you would think that would be enough space for every car that my husband had since at this point in our lives he was repairing cars that had mechanical issues and reselling them. However, I came home from work one evening and found the nose of a 1984 Oldsmobile Cutlass in my dining room. Need I say more.

Be prudent with your purchases in life. Don't go overboard and don't allow you desires to get the best of you. Some of those desires can lead you straight to hell especially adultery and alcohol.

Chapter Twenty Eight

Proverbs 28:1

"The wicked flee when no man pursueth: but the righteous are bold as a lion."

There is an old saying "tell the truth and shame the devil." - Francois Rabelais

"Silence becomes cowardice when occasion demands speaking out the whole truth and acting accordingly." - Mahatma Gandhi

Truth is like the sun. You can shut it out for a time, but it ain't goin' away. –Elvis Presley.

Truth will always be truth, regardless of lack of understanding, disbelief or ignorance. –W. Clement Stone.

We learned about honesty and integrity - that the truth matters... that you don't take shortcuts or play by your own set of rules... and success doesn't count unless you earn it fair and square. –Michelle Obama.

The truth is incontrovertible. Malice may attack it, ignorance may deride it, but in the end, there it is. –Winston Churchill.

Truth is powerful, and it prevails. –Sojourner Truth

I never did give anybody hell. I just told the truth, and they thought it was hell. –Harry S. Truman.

Wherefore putting away lying, speak every man truth with his neighbour: for we are members one of another. –Ephesians 4:25

The integrity of the upright shall guide them: but the perverseness of transgressors shall destroy them. –Proverbs 11:3

A faithful witness will not lie: but a false witness will utter lies. – Proverbs 14:5

"Finally, brethren, whatsoever things are true, whatsoever things are honest, whatsoever things are just, whatsoever things are pure, whatsoever things are lovely, whatsoever things are of good report; if there be any virtue, and if there be any praise, think on these things."–Philippians 4:8

What value do you place on the truth? Would you characterize your life as a quest for things truthful? "The wicked flee when no man purseuth: but the righteous are bold as a lion."–Proverbs 28:1. The reason people flee is that they have a bad conscience. Let's use this as an example. If you are driving and you look in your rear-view mirror and see a police car but even worse, you see a police car ahead of you what is your reaction? Are you comfortable and relaxed or do you become fearful and nervous? If you are living a righteous life and doing things correctly and you have insurance, your registration is current, your inspection is up to date, you have a license and it's valid, you're not under the influence, you're not smuggling narcotics, etc.

"If you tell the truth, then you don't have to have a good memory."–Judge Judy Sheindlin.

160

Proverbs 28:9

"He that turneth away his ear from hearing the law, even his prayer shall be abomination."

Do you rejoice in the word? Do you read your bible daily? Do you carry your Bible with you to church? Do you attend church services on a weekly basis? Do you pray daily? When the preacher delivers a sermon do you meditate on it to see how it applies to your life?

Ministers are the Lord's authorized representatives. God delivers his word to them to give you to help you live the abundant life he wants for you. If you refuse to listen to the preacher with the word that God has given him for you then God will close his ears when you pray and ask him for things. God is shocked and appalled by our lack of listening and obeying. It horrifies the Lord that we would turn a deaf ear to what He has said. God considers such things an abomination! When we do not obey the word, God considers our prayers an abomination.

We are living in the last days and we all need to turn to God. We need to attend church and we need to pray daily. "This book of the law shall not depart out of thy mouth; but thou shalt meditate therein day and night, that thou mayest observe to do according to all that is written therein: for then thou shalt make thy way prosperous, and then thou shalt have good success."–Joshua 1:8.

Many churches today have multiple services per week. The church I attend has two services on Sundays, one on Wednesday, and one on Saturday evening. There is really no reason you cannot attend church. Sure, sometimes you may be sick at home or hospitalized but even then, most people have a tablet or cell phone where they can see a church service on TV.

The same way we are diligent in going to work every day we should to be diligent in our relationship with God daily. The same way we invest time to learn our jobs thoroughly, so we can get promotions is the same way we have to invest time in God's word daily and he will promote us in ways we could never imagine.

Don't treat God like he is on the sideline, God must always be the mainline!

Proverbs 28:13

"He that covereth his sins shall not prosper: but whoso confesseth and forsaketh them shall have mercy."

The way in which you manage your sins is important. "If you confess them, he is faithful and just to forgive you. If we confess our sins, he is faithful and just to forgive us our sins, and to cleanse us from all unrighteousness."–1 John 1:9.

When we sin, our natural tendency is to conceal the sin. This natural tendency came from the Garden of Eden with Adam and Eve. "And the eyes of them both were opened, and they knew that they were naked; and they sewed fig leaves together and made themselves aprons. And the Lord God called unto Adam, and said unto him, Where art thou? And he said, I heard thy voice in the garden, and I was afraid, because I was naked; and I hid myself. And he said, who told thee that thou wast naked? Hast thou eaten of the tree, whereof I commanded thee that thou shouldest not eat? And the man said, the woman whom thou gavest to be with me, she gave me of the tree, and I did eat." Genesis 3:7-12. What Adam and Eve did resulted in them being unprosperous.

God's forgiveness is unending. When you confess your sins to God and really are sorry, he will forgive you. God does not think or operate on our level he has a greater understanding. "Seek ye the Lord while he may be found, call ye upon him while he is near: Let the wicked forsake his way, and the unrighteous man his thoughts: and let him return unto the Lord, and he will have mercy upon him; and to our God, for he will abundantly pardon. For my thoughts are not your thoughts, neither are your ways my ways, saith the Lord. For as the heavens are higher than the earth, so are my ways higher than your ways, and my thoughts than your thoughts."–Isaiah 55:6-9.

Proverbs 28:24

"Whoso robbeth his father or his mother, and saith, it is no transgression; the same is the companion of a destroyer."

He who robs his parents is worse than a common robber. Along with the cruel act he or she has committed against his parents they also add ingratitude, cruelty, and disobedience. Any child that would commit such a sin against their parents is in the same category as a child that would commit parricide.

Children can steal from their parents in many ways. One of the obvious ways is to steal any money they find. They can also steal any checks that their parents have received by forging the parent's name and cashing the check. Then there is jewelry. If they can get

163

their hands on any they can take it and go to the nearest pawn shop. The amazing thing about all of this is the child's mindset. They believe there is nothing wrong with what they are doing because they feel everything their parents own belong to them. Then they have a dangerous mindset, if I get caught, my parents won't press charges. Whenever a child commits a crime against his parents, society doesn't see it that way.

Stealing from a parent is a very heinous case of theft. One of the Ten Commandments states "Thou Shalt Not Steal."–Exodus 20:15. While they do not consider crimes of this type being a big deal where society is concerned it is a big deal with God. The Lord will judge such acts with severity.

Such perverse acts will not mock God. "Be not deceived; God is not mocked: for whatsoever a man soweth, that shall he also reap."–Galatians 6:7. "The eye that mocketh at his father, and despiseth to obey his mother, the ravens of the valley shall pick it out, and the young eagles shall eat it."–Proverbs 30:17.

Remember another of the Ten Commandments, "Honour thy father and thy mother: that thy days may be long upon the land which the Lord thy God giveth thee."–Exodus 20:12.

Chapter Twenty Nine

Proverbs 29:2

"When the righteous are in authority, the people rejoice: but when the wicked beareth rule, the people mourn."

This proverb speaks about politics and the people in power. The first part of this proverb speaks about when the righteous become great, or when they are in authority.

In the book of Esther, King Ahasuerus promoted a man called Haman. The people were upset to hear of the advancement. Mordecai who was Esther's cousin was a godly and righteous man. Now King Ahasuerus wife Vashti was a disappointment to him, and his servants advised him to look for a new wife. The king agreed, and the servants began immediately to seek young virgins to send to the king. They advised Mordecai of this and he sent Esther even though she was a Jew like Mordecai. All the young virgins had to undergo a purification process which lasted one year. When it was Esther's turn, she went into King Ahasuerus and the king loved her more than the others and placed the royal crown on her head and she became the new queen. When the king was advised of Haman's plot to kill all the Jewish people, he declared that Haman should be hung on the gallows he planned to hang

Mordecai on. Once Mordecai took over Haman's position the people were elated.

We should look for godly men and women to be in power. The issue we have is that we don't insist on godly leaders! We don't advise all parties we will endure nothing less. What we need are godly people to lead us. People who desire the best for our country the United States as well as all international countries the people should demand nothing less from their leaders as well. We are living in a time right now where hate and division is conquering our polls. Until we come together and get unified, we will continue to agonize because wicked people are in power and we placed them there.

Proverbs 29:11

"A fool uttereth all his mind: but a wise man keepeth it in till afterwards."

In 2003 they released a movie called "Anger Management". It had an all-star cast with a budget of $83.5 million and ultimately had a worldwide gross of $195,745,823 after being in the theatres for 19 weeks. The plot of the movie revolved around a man who had an embarrassing event happen to him in public and that left a lasting trauma about public affection and repressing his emotions. While in route via plane to a business meeting several irritating events took place, and this man lost his temper got locked up and then was sentenced to anger management therapy.

Anger can be very destructive and get you into a lot of trouble. Anger can be a difficult thing to control because too often it is upon us before we realize it. The reason we become angry is that we cannot control the situation at hand. When we react like this, it shows that we are not content to submit ourselves to God. "Humble yourselves in the sight of the Lord, and he shall lift you up."–James 4:10.

There is a time and place for everything. Therefore, there is a time to speak and a time to be silent. "A time to rend, and a time to sew; a time to keep silence, and a time to speak."–Ecclesiastes 3:7. A wise person knows how to restrain their speech. Wise people choose their words carefully and give thought to what they will say before they speak. A fool loves to hear himself speak and because of that finds himself or herself in many a precarious situations. "Even so the tongue is a little member, and boasteth great things. Behold, how great a matter a little fire kindleth! And the tongue is a fire, a world of iniquity: so is the tongue among our members, that it defileth the whole body, and setteth on fire the course of nature; and it is set on fire of hell. For every kind of beasts, and of birds, and of serpents, and of things in the sea, is tamed, and hath been tamed of mankind: But the tongue can no man tame; it is an unruly evil, full of deadly poison. Therewith bless we God, even the Father; and therewith curse we men, which are made after the similitude of God. Out of the same mouth proceedeth blessing and cursing. My brethren, these things ought not so to be. Doth a fountain send forth at the same place sweet water and bitter? Can the fig tree, my brethren, bear olive berries? either a vine, figs? so can no fountain both yield salt water and fresh."–James 3:5-12.

So, if the bible says the tongue no man can tame, and that gets us into trouble and raises our anger when we don't get our way what do we do? We pray and ask God for help and remember, "I can do all things through Christ which strengtheneth me."–Philippians 4:13.

Proverbs 29:18

"Where there is no vision, the people perish: but he that keepeth the law, happy is he."

Where there are no laws and guidance there will be no restraint. A perfect example is traffic signals. As a driver, you know or should know green means go, yellow means yield, and red means stop. Now you have many people who do things their way. When that happens that is how you have accidents on the road. People who don't stop at a stop sign. People who turned right on a red arrow instead of waiting for the arrow to change to green. Then you have the ones who apparently don't have a brake pedal on their car and zoom through the school zones instead of driving 20 mph.

Where there is no vision and laws destructive things happen. We see that with the children of Israel when Moses went up into the mountains to receive the tablets with the Ten Commandments. The children of Israel became morally and spiritually out of control. They made their own God out of gold and worshipped it while Moses was away. They became so unruly, wouldn't listen to Aaron and by the time Moses returned it looked like they were having an orgy in camp.

That says a lot. Where there is an absence of the word of God only bad things will happen. "Thy word is a lamp unto my feet, and a light unto my path."–Psalm 119:105.

We all need God's word. God's word is a great blessing. Without the word of God to save us, people will worship anything and everything. Treasure God's word obey what you read and hear from the bible and you will have a blessed life.

Book of Proverbs

Chapter Thirty

Proverbs 30:25

"The ants are a people not strong, yet they prepare their meat in the summer."

Ants are smart creatures. Ants have and display wisdom that many people do not have. The work ethic of the ant is incredible. The way they proceed in a single line from a source of food to where they want to store it until they have taken every bit.

Ants are extremely feeble however they rely on wisdom to maintain and defend themselves. Ants flourish due to their wisdom. Ants work profusely in the summer to procure their food supply that they eat in the Autumn and Spring seasons underground. The wisdom of the ant is how he prepares when he can for a time when he will need what he has prepared. This makes ants exceedingly wise.

Do you have the wisdom of an ant or can they teach you something? Do you have a savings account? Are you preparing for the future? In this life, we need to be wise in preparing for the future as best we can. You need to understand that the example of the ants is that he works hard when he can to provide.

People with wisdom do not spend all their income. Paying your bills is important because you are paying for services that have been rendered to you. However, when you put money into savings, you are paying yourself. The first 10% of your income belongs to God. The dictionary defines the word "tithe" as "a tenth part of something. "Will a man rob God? Yet ye have robbed me. But ye say, wherein have we robbed thee? In tithes and offerings. Ye are cursed with a curse: for ye have robbed me, even this whole nation. Bring ye all the tithes into the storehouse, that there may be meat in mine house, and prove me now herewith, saith the Lord of hosts, if I will not open you the windows of heaven, and pour you out a blessing, that there shall not be room enough to receive it. And I will rebuke the devourer for your sakes, and he shall not destroy the fruits of your ground; neither shall your vine cast her fruit before the time in the field, saith the Lord of hosts. And all nations shall call you blessed: for ye shall be a delightsome land, saith the Lord of hosts."–Malachi 3:8-12.

After you give God the first 10% then you pay yourself the second 10% and the rest is for you to live off. This is a recipe for success and God will bless you. Isn't it amazing how one of the smallest creatures can teach us one of King Solomon's greatest priceless proverbs of wisdom?

Proverbs 30:33

"Surely the churning of milk bringeth forth butter, and the wringing of the nose bringeth forth blood: so, the forcing of wrath bringeth forth strife."

Nobody can deny the first two parts of this proverb. The first is the churning of butter. When milk is put into a butter churn, it is a liquid. However, after a period it will separate into butter and buttermilk. Regarding the wringing of the nose you cannot just press down on a nose for it to bleed you have to twist it hard and the blood vessels will break, and blood will flow from the nose.

The reason these two examples have preceded this one is that God wants us to know the churning of anger will produce strife. Angry responses cause strife. Angry people are dangerous people. When you are angry, then you plot evil and revenge and then strife rears its ugly head. Once the plotting of the first party has is completed then the person who is plotted against becomes furious and then the strife between the two will last for an indefinite amount of time.

Everyone gets angry but people who have wisdom just let it go and move on. Wise people are slow to wrath and realize what it can lead to if they don't control themselves. "The discretion of a man deferreth his anger; and it is his glory to pass over a transgression."–Proverbs 19:11. "Wherefore, my beloved brethren, let every man be swift to hear, slow to speak, slow to wrath."–James 1:19. "Be ye angry, and sin not: let not the sun go down upon your wrath."–Ephesians 4:26. Ladies this verse exemplifies us often regarding our mates. When we get upset with them, then we stop speaking and most times they spend the night on the sofa or in their man cave or anywhere else except the bedroom. This is one I have had to work on for a while.

We are to gain control over our anger and don't let it brew or boil. Anger does not please God, and it does not help us health wise. Anger weakens our liver and we know how vital our liver is to us. Anger can; lead to murder and we see how Cain murdered Able in the bible. "Ye have heard that it was said of them of old time, thou shalt not kill; and whosoever shall kill shall be in danger of the judgment: But I say unto you, That whosoever is angry with his brother without a cause shall be in danger of the judgment: and whosoever shall say to his brother, Raca, shall be in danger of the council: but whosoever shall say, Thou fool, shall be in danger of hell fire."–Matthew 5:21-22.

Life is too short to indulge in anger. "Ye have heard that it hath been said, thou shalt love thy neighbour, and hate thine enemy. But I say unto you, Love your enemies, bless them that curse you, do good to them that hate you, and pray for them which despitefully use you, and persecute you; That ye may be the children of your Father which is in heaven: for he maketh his sun to rise on the evil and on the good, and sendeth rain on the just and on the unjust. For if ye love them which love you, what reward have ye? Do not even the publicans the same? And if ye salute your brethren only, what do ye more than others? do not even the publicans so? Be ye therefore perfect, even as your Father which is in heaven is perfect."–Matthew 5:43-48.

Chapter Thirty One

Proverbs 31:20

"She stretcheth out her hand to the poor; yea, she reacheth forth her hands to the needy."

The woman that proverbs is describing in this verse is a giver. Her hands are always open, available, free to give to the poor. This woman doesn't just have her family on her mind she also reaches out to the poor and needy as well.

This type of woman is always accessible. Even though her dedication is to her family, she stretches herself more by volunteering for charity work. This woman doesn't focus on herself she places her focus on others. Because of these reasons a virtuous woman is commended by all.

A virtuous woman is loved by all and praised by husband and children. "Now there was at Joppa a certain disciple named Tabitha, which by interpretation is called Dorcas: this woman was full of good works and almsdeeds which she did. And it came to pass in those days, that she was sick, and died: whom when they had washed, they laid her in an upper chamber. And forasmuch as Lydda was nigh to Joppa, and the disciples had heard that Peter was there, they sent unto him two men, desiring him that he would not delay to come to them. Then Peter arose and went with them. When he was come, they brought him into the upper chamber: and all the widows stood by him weeping, and shewing the coats and garments which Dorcas made, while she was with them. But Peter put them all forth, and kneeled down, and prayed; and turning him to the body said, Tabitha, arise. And she opened her eyes: and when she saw Peter, she sat up. And he gave her his hand, and lifted her up, and when he had called the saints and widows, presented her alive. And it was known throughout all Joppa; and many believed in the Lord."–Acts 9:36-42.

Women, do you reach out to help others? Are your hands open to the poor, or are you close-fisted with your possessions? Do you willingly reach out to find and give to those who are in need?

Proverbs 31:26

"She openeth her mouth with wisdom; and in her tongue is the law of kindness."

An excellent wife is one whose words are a blessing to all those who hear them. A virtuous woman is graceful in speech and action and she is admired and given recognition. People realize that as soon as her mouth opens to speak wisdom pours forth from it.

A virtuous woman knows the right words for any celebration. This woman is careful and only speaks after examining her answer to a question or problem. This woman carefully thinks through her responses before she responds to questions or problems. A virtuous woman will use wisdom before she opens her mouth even though she has her own skills and achievements. Even with her own abilities and accomplishments, she is still wise and kind in her speech.

A virtuous woman will build you up when you are distraught, commend you when negative people try to tear you down, and take time to reminisce with you about past times to revitalize you.

In the Bible there is the story of a woman named Ruth. They called Ruth a virtuous woman. "And now, my daughter, fear not; I will do to thee all that thou requirest: for all the city of my people doth know that thou art a virtuous woman."–Ruth 3:13.

The book of Ruth reflects the love, commitment, loss, and fortitude of this woman. Ruth was a direct ancestor of Lot who was Abraham's nephew and a gentile. Ruth had many challenges in her life. Her husband passed away, she never had children, and she was living with her widowed mother-in-law. Ruth embodied loyal love. Ruth was a woman of noble character. After the death of her husband, Ruth stayed with her mother-in-law Naomi and traveled wherever she went. Ruth had great faith. Her faith and belief in God that he would provide for Naomi and herself was solid. They introduced Ruth to a man named Boaz, and she proved to be a woman of integrity with Boaz. Ruth showed incredible character in obscurity. Boaz was a single wealthy man and Ruth went to work for him in the fields. Boaz fell in love with Ruth and she went from a lowly field worker to being Boaz's wife. The book of Ruth shows the workings of divine providence. The book reveals the extent of God's grace. God fully accepted Ruth into His elect people and recognized her with a role in continuing the family line into which his appointed king, David, and later His Son, Jesus, would be born. After Boaz married Ruth, she became pregnant and had a son they named Obed. This man Obed became the father of Jesse. Now Jesse was the father of David who was in the direct family line of Jesus Christ.

Notes

Introduction

Oprah Winfrey quote from Goodreeds.com

Tim Fargo quote from Goodreeds.com

Barack Obama quote from Goodreeds.com

Jimi Hendrix quote from BrainyQuote.com

Charles De Lint quote from Goodreeds.com

Leonardo Da Vinci quote from Goodreeds.com

Billy Graham quote from QuoteMountain.com

Bob Marley quote from Goodreeds.com

Goldie Hawn quote from Goodreeds.com

Chapter 1

Proverbs 1:5

Proverbs 1:7

Proverbs 1:22

Proverbs 1:26

Proverbs 1:31

Psalm 2:4

Psalm 37:13

Exodus 20:12

All Bible references are from the Kings James Bible

All Dictionary references are from Merriam-Webster

Chapter 2

Proverbs 2:3

Proverbs 2:7

Proverbs 2:11

Matthew 7:7

1 Kings 3:3-14

1 Chronicle 5:18

Song of Solomon 4:4

Chapter 3

Proverbs 3:3

Proverbs 3:5

Proverbs 3:6

Proverbs 3:9

Proverbs 3:16

Proverbs 3:27

Proverbs 10:4

Proverbs 27:18

Matthew 5:38-42

Matthew 6:33

Matthew 26:11

Malachi 3:8-12

Roman 13:7-8

All Bible References are from the King James Bible

All Dictionary references are from Merriam-Webster

Og Mandino quote from BrainyQuote.com

Elizabeth Cady Stanton quote from Goodreeds.com

Oliver Herford quote from Goodreeds.com

Chapter 4

Proverbs 4:5

Proverbs 4:6

Proverbs 4:7

Proverbs 4:8

Proverbs 4:13

Proverbs 4:24

Proverbs 17:28

Ephesians 4:29

Hebrews 12:2

Luke 23;34

Matthew 12:34

All Bible references are from the Kings James Bible

All Dictionary references are from Merriam-Webster

Chapter 5

Proverbs 5:18

Proverbs 5:19

Proverbs 5:20

Mark 10:9

Colossians 3:19

All Bible references are from the Kings James Bible

All Dictionary references are from Merriam-Webster

Chapter 6

Proverbs 6:9

Proverbs 6:17

Proverbs 6:18

Proverbs 6:19

Proverbs 6:23

Proverbs 6:32

Exodus 20:6

Matthew 5:9

Genesis 1:16

All Bible references are from the Kings James Bible

All Dictionary references are from Merriam-Webster

C.S. Lewis quote from Goodreeds.com

Andrew Murray quote from Goodreeds.com

Aldert Vrij quote from Scientific American September 1, 2011 issue by Wray Herbert

Chapter 7

Proverbs 7:2

Proverbs 7:26

Proverbs 7:27

John 3:16

All Bible references are from the Kings James Bible

All Dictionary references are from Merriam-Webster

Albert Einstein quote from Goodreeds.com

Chapter 8

Proverbs 8:10

Proverbs 8:11

Proverbs 8:13

Proverbs 8:18

Proverbs 8:19

Proverbs 8:21

Proverbs 8:34

Proverbs 8:35

Proverbs 8:36

1 Corinthians 3:16

All Bible references are from the Kings James Bible

All Dictionary references are from Merriam-Webster

Chapter 9

Proverbs 9:6

Proverbs 9:9

Proverbs 9:10

Proverbs 9:11

Chapter 10

Proverbs 10:2

Proverbs 10:3

Proverbs 10:4

Proverbs 10:6

Proverbs 10:12

Proverbs 10:15

Proverbs 10:21

Proverbs 10:22

Proverbs 10:25

Proverbs 10:27

Matthew 6:15

Ephesians 4:32

Luke 6:27

Luke 6:37

Deuteronomy 15:10

John 16:33

Exodus 12:7

Exodus 12:12-13

All Bible references are from the Kings James Bible

All Dictionary references are from Merriam-Webster

Chapter 11

Proverbs 11:2

Proverbs 11:13

Proverbs 11:24

Proverbs 11:28

Psalm 121:1

Matthew 6:24

Matthew 23:12

John 5:19

Luke 8:11

1 King 3:9-13

Luke 6:38

Mark 4:19

All Bible references are from the Kings James Bible

All Dictionary references are from Merriam-Webster

Chapter 12

Proverbs 12:2

Proverbs 12:4

Proverbs 12:14

Proverbs 12:21

1 Corinthians 12:27

1 Corinthians 12:14-23

Matthew 12:36-37

Joel 3:10

Ephesians 6:10-12

All Bible references are from the Kings James Bible

All Dictionary references are from Merriam-Webster

Chapter 13

Proverbs 13:7

Proverbs 13:13

Proverbs 13:22

Proverbs 13:24

Hebrews 12:5-7

All Bible references are from the Kings James Bible

All Dictionary references are from Merriam-Webster

Smith Wigglesworth quote from Goodreeds.com

Chapter 14

Proverbs 14:7

Proverbs 14:17

Proverbs 14:25

Proverbs 14:26

Proverbs 14:29

Psalm 14:1

Psalm 34:7

Daniel 3:10-28

Ecclesiates 7:9

Matthew 7:26-27

All Bible references are from the Kings James Bible

All Dictionary references are from Merriam-Webster

Chapter 15

Proverbs 15:3

Proverbs 15:4

Proverbs 15:15

Proverbs 15:22

Romans 8:11

2 Timothy 1:14

2 Chronicles 16:9

All Bible references are from the Kings James Bible

All Dictionary references are from Merriam-Webster

Amazon Echo quote from The Mercury News May 25 2018 by Levi Sumagaysay

Chapter 16

Proverbs 16:3

Proverbs 16:7

Proverbs 16:17

Proverbs 16:20

Mark 4:37-41

2 Chronicles 1:7-12

Matthew 21:22

Hebrews 11:1

1 Corinthians 2:5

All Bible references are from the Kings James Bible

All Dictionary references are from Merriam-Webster

Chapter 17

Proverbs 17:5

Proverbs 17:9

Proverbs 17:15

Proverbs 17:25

Proverbs 17:28

Matthew 7:12

James 1:17

All Bible references are from the Kings James Bible

All Dictionary references are from Merriam-Webster

Story of The Turtle Who Couldn't Stop Talking from The Panchatantram collection of fables from India 300 CE

Chapter 18

Proverbs 18:4

Proverbs 18:20

Proverbs 18:21

Proverbs 18:22

Genesis 2:18

Geneses 2:21-24

All Bible references are from the Kings James Bible

All Dictionary references are from Merriam-Webster

Chapter 19

Proverbs 19:1

Proverbs 19:17

Proverbs 19:18

Proverbs 19:24

Proverbs 11:24-26

Proverbs 22-6

Proverbs 13:24

Ephesians 6:4

Luke 6:38

1 Samuel 25:2-3

All Bible references are from the Kings James Bible

All Dictionary references are from Merriam-Webster

Chapter 20

Proverbs 20:1

Proverbs 20:9

Proverbs 20:20

Proverbs 20:29

Psalm 104:15

Ephesians 5:18

Ecclesiastes 7:20

Job 1:1

Romans 12:19

Ezekiel 25:17

Hebrews 10:30

1 Thessalonians 5:15

All Bible references are from the Kings James Bible

All Dictionary references are from Merriam-Webster

Chapter 21

Proverbs 21:6

Proverbs 21:9

Proverbs 21:16

Hebrews 4:13

Matthew 7:24-27

All Bible references are from the Kings James Bible

All Dictionary references are from Merriam-Webster

Chapter 22

Proverbs 22:4

Proverbs 22:7

Proverbs 22:9

Proverbs 22:17

Proverbs 16:7

Proverbs 11:25

1 Peter 5:6-7

Psalm 41:1-3

Ephesians 3:20-21

Romans 12;3

All Bible references are from the Kings James Bible

All Dictionary references are from Merriam-Webster

Chapter 23

Proverbs 23:4

Proverbs 23:5

Proverbs 23:12

Proverbs 23:23

1 Timothy 6:7

1 Timothy 6:10

Luke 12:16-21

Job 1:21

Matthew 6:19-21

Ecclesiastes 2:24

Ecclesiastes 3:13

All Bible references are from the Kings James Bible

All Dictionary references are from Merriam-Webster

Chapter 24

Proverbs 24:10

Proverbs 24:12

Proverbs 24:16

Proverbs 24:29

Proverbs 22:13

Philippians 4:13

Psalm 34:19

Romans 12:19-21

All Bible references are from the Kings James Bible

All Dictionary references are from Merriam-Webster

Winston Churchill quotes from Goodreeds.com

Chapter 25

Proverbs 25:11

Proverbs 25:19

Proverbs 25:21

Proverbs 25:22

Psalm 27:10

Psalm 46

Matthew 5:44-45

Luke 10:30-37

All Bible references are from the Kings James Bible

All Dictionary references are from Merriam-Webster

Chapter 26

Proverbs 26:4

Proverbs 26:11

Proverbs 26:20

Proverbs 26:27

Matthew 7:6

Proverbs 14:7

Proverbs 6:12

Romans 12;19

Psalm 7:15-16

All Bible references are from the Kings James Bible

All Dictionary references are from Merriam-Webster

Chapter 27

Proverbs 27:1

Proverbs 27:2

Proverbs 27:20

Psalm 118:24

Psalm 150:6

Psalm 113:1-3

James 4:13-16

Isaiah 43:21

Matthew 6:25-34

Matthew 12:34

1 Corinthians 13:4-7

1 John 2:15-16

1 Timothy 6:6

Genesis 3:6

All Bible references are from the Kings James Bible

All Dictionary references are from Merriam-Webster

Chapter 28

Proverbs 28:1

Proverbs 28:9

Proverbs 28:13

Proverbs 28:24

Ephesians 4:25

Proverbs 11:3

Proverbs 14:5

Proverbs 30:17

Philippians 4:8

Joshua 1:8

1 John 1:19

Geneses 3:7-12

Isaiah 55:5-9

Exodus 20:12

Exodus 20:15

Galatians 6:7

All Bible references are from the Kings James Bible

All Dictionary references are from Merriam-Webster

Mahatma Gandhi quote from Goodreeds.com

Elvis Presley quote from Goodreeds.com

W. Clement Stone quote from Goodreeds.com

Michelle Obama quote from BrainyQuote.com

Winston Churchill quote from Goodreeds.com

Sojourner Truth quote from Brainyquote.com

Harry S. Truman quote from BrainyQuote.com

Chapter 29

Proverbs 29:2

Proverbs 29:11

Proverbs 29:18

James 4:10

James 3:5-12

Ecclesiastes 3:7

Philippians 4:13

Psalm 119:105

All Bible references are from the Kings James Bible

All Dictionary references are from Merriam-Webster

Chapter 30

Proverbs 30:25

Proverbs 30:33

Proverbs 19:11

Ephesians 4:26

Malachi 3:8-12

James 1:19

Matthew 5:21-22

Matthew 5:43-48

All Bible references are from the Kings James Bible

All Dictionary references are from Merriam-Webster

Chapter 31

Proverbs 31:20

Proverbs 31:26

Acts 9:36-42

Ruth 3:13

All Bible references are from the Kings James Bible

All Dictionary references are from Merriam-Webster

About the Author

Raised in New York, Donna Louis has always had a penchant for writing. Constantly surrounded by pen and paper Donna studied writing courses at Queensboro Community College in New York. She attended The Institute of Children's Writers and Long Ridge Writers Group in Connecticut. She moved to Florida and because of her relationship with The Holy Spirit she wrote a book on miracles.

Donna's first book Miracles of Direction Miracles of Conquest Miracles of Provision Miracles of Purpose helped readers explore miracles both past and present. The book explores biblical miracles that took place while Jesus was here on earth. She then references with miracles that take place daily in the modern world. She separates these miracles into four categories and presents insightful examples of each type, taken directly from the Bible.

They chose her as the winner in the 2018 Top Female Author Awards in the Religion/Philosophy/Spiritual category from The Author Show. They chose Donna from an international field of contestants by a panel of judges. They also chose her as a winner in 50 Great Writers You Should Be Reading in 2015, 2016, 2017 and 2018.

Donna Louis' second book best-selling book, 'Thriving in Every Season of Life with God', gives us a road map to create a mindset - a new life in which we can learn to prosper in any circumstance, however dire. The book achieved bestseller status in two categories: Spiritual Self Help and Motivational Self Help.

Donna has been married to her husband of 37 years Patrick Louis and lives in Florida. She lives to accomplish the task that God created her for and daily to follow Proverbs 3:5-6. "Trust in the Lord with all thine heart and lean not unto thine own understanding. In all thy ways acknowledge him, and he shall direct thy paths."

Made in the USA
Columbia, SC
19 November 2024

46486639R00117